THE BOOK OF
MENTORS
HONORING
JIM ROHN

CREATED BY MULTI #1 INTERNATIONAL BESTSELLING AUTHOR & AWARD WINNING SPEAKER ON HABITS

ERIK "MR AWESOME" SWANSON

THE BOOK OF
MENTORS

Keys To Success Honoring Legacy
Legends Zig Ziglar, Bob Proctor,
Dr. Wayne Dyer, & Jim Rohn

HONORING
JIM ROHN

Copyright © 2025

THE BOOK OF MENTORS

Orders by U.S. trade bookstores and wholesalers.

Email: *Team@IntegrityPub.com*

Manufactured and printed in the United States of America and distributed globally by Integrity Pub.

Hardback ISBN: 978-1-964330-19-8
Paperback ISBN: 978-1-964330-18-1

Celebrity Testimonials

THE BOOK OF MENTORS

The Book of Mentors ~ Honoring Legacy Legends Zig Ziglar, Bob Proctor, Dr. Wayne Dyer, and Jim Rohn!

"Bravo, Bravo, Bravo! I want to compliment you in deciding to find a Mentor in your life. We all need them!"

Sir Bruno Serato ~ Philanthropist, Founder of Caterina's Club, CNN Man of the Year, Bestselling Author, Owner and Chef of the Anaheim White House ~ www.AnaheimWhitehouse.com

"A true mentor can offer you invaluable insights and advice that will help you navigate challenges and opportunities throughout your life."

Brian Tracy ~ Author, Speaker, Motivator ~ www.BrianTracy.com

"I changed directions, but I never changed the dream!"

Rudy Ruettiger ~ Author, Speaker, Inspirational Mentor, The Real Rudy from the movie 'RUDY' ~ www.RudyRuettiger.com

"Mentorship is life! Increase your world by learning from those who have stepped into greatness before you, and then strive to become a Mentor to those who follow you in your footsteps in the future."

Erik "Mr. Awesome" Swanson ~ Author, Speaker, Habits Coach ~ www.SpeakerErikSwanson.com

"There are two ways to learn. One is from the books we read and the other is being around smarter people. We become the average of the people we spend most of our time with People who do not read are no better off than people who cannot read to quote Mark Twain."

Don Green ~ President of the Napoleon Hill Foundation, Author, Speaker, Mentor ~ www.NapHill.org

"Be curious about your available sources of mentorship. There is often much to learn from those we perceive as less experienced."

Paul Blanchard ~ Author, Speaker, Habits Coach ~ www.WholeBodyMindset.com

"Success isn't the Gold Medal. It's the Silver Medal. The Gold Medal is significance. You achieve significance by helping someone else succeed. That is true mentorship!"

Ruben Gonzalez ~ Author, Speaker, Four-Time Olympian ~ www.TheLugeMan.com

"I have had some great mentors when I first started in the media business in NYC, that allowed me to take on some very tricky assignments at a very young age. Since then, I have been mentoring folks on a regular basis and it is incredibly satisfying to see them grow and succeed not only in business but also in their personal lives."

Larry Namer ~ Founder of E! Entertainment Television ~ www.EOnline.com

"Mentors are the teachers of life. 'If you give a man a fish, you feed him for a day. If you teach a man to fish, you feed him for a lifetime.' The mentors of life will perpetually become the heart and soul of progress and evolution in our world."

Jon Kovach Jr. ~ Author, Speaker, Mastermind Leader ~ www.SpeakerJonKovachJr.com

"Mentorship is a bridge between your VISION and its manifestation. It's having a Confidant by your side, who recognizes your greatness, and casts LIGHT on the path to accessing your Highest Self, and most elevated potential. Embracing the guidance of a mentor will INSPIRE and EMPOWER you to transform the ordinary into TRIUMPH. This sacred relationship evokes your BRILLIANCE, so you navigate through mists of uncertainty to the shores of CLARITY and ACHIEVEMENT."

Niurka ~ Transformation & Fulfillment Coach, NLP Master ~ www.NiurkaInc.com

"The gap between your divine potential and where you are today is called mentorship."

Darryll Stinson ~ Entrepreneur, Pastor, Speaker, Suicide Survivor ~ www.DarryllStinson.com

"A mentor is a great encourager. Mentorship is teaching from experience but deciding how to impart those lessons to others at the right times. Mentorship is all about experience that is shared with others. Then they encourage you to pursue the advice given."

Don Hobbs ~ Former President Success Magazine, Named Best Marketer by Tony Robbins, Co-Founder 7 Figure Coaching Secrets ~ www.DonHobbs.com

Global Speakers Mastermind & Habitude Warrior Masterminds

Join us and become a member of our tribe! Our Global Speakers Mastermind is a virtual group of amazing thinkers and leaders who meet twice a month. Sessions are designed to be 'to the point' and focused while sharing fantastic techniques to grow your mindset as well as your pocketbooks. We also include famous guest speaker spots for our private Masterclasses. We also designate certain sessions for our members to mastermind with each other & and counsel on the topics discussed in our previous Masterclasses. It's time for you to join a tribe who truly cares about **YOU** and your future and start surrounding yourself with the famous leaders and mentors of our time. It is time for you to up-level your life, businesses, and relationships.

For more information to check out our Masterminds:
Team@HabitudeWarrior.com
www.DecideToBeAwesome.com

BECOME AN INTERNATIONAL
#1 BESTSELLING AUTHOR & SPEAKER

Habitude Warrior International has been highlighting award-winning Speakers and #1 Bestselling Authors for over 25 years. They know what it takes to become #1 in your field and how to get the best exposure around the world. If you have ever considered giving yourself the GIFT of becoming a well-known Speaker and a fantastically well known #1 Best-Selling Author, then you should email their team right away to find out more information in how you can become involved. They have the best of the best when it comes to resources in achieving the bestselling status in your particular field. Start surrounding yourself with the N.Y. Times Bestsellers of our time and start seeing your dreams become reality!

For more information to become a #1 Bestselling Author & Speaker on our Habitude Warrior Conferences Please text the word AUTHORS to 619-304-6268 And also go to:
www.DecideToBeAwesome.com

Acknowledgement To Jim Rohn

With immense respect and profound appreciation, I, along with the extraordinary team of co-authors in this series, extend our heartfelt gratitude to the legendary Jim Rohn. His timeless wisdom and unwavering dedication to personal growth, leadership, and mentorship have profoundly impacted countless lives worldwide.

Jim Rohn's transformative teachings and insights—captured in his iconic works such as *The Seasons of Life* and *Leading an Inspired Life*—continue to serve as guiding lights for those seeking purpose, excellence, and success. His mentorship has empowered generations to strive for greatness, live with intention, and cultivate the habits and principles that lead to enduring achievement. Through his words, teachings, and influence, Jim Rohn has created a legacy of empowerment.

With the deepest respect, we honor Jim Rohn for the remarkable impact he has had on the world and on our lives. May his teachings continue to guide and inspire us to reach new heights and to make a meaningful difference in the lives of others.

~ Erik "Mr. Awesome" Swanson ~ Multi #1 International Bestselling Author & Award-Winning Speaker

CONTENTS

HONORING JIM ROHN

Introduction

THE BOOK OF MENTORS

Welcome to *The Book of Mentor*s book series—an extraordinary journey of transformation, guidance, and wisdom. In the pages that follow, you will find a riveting exploration of mentorship, leadership, and the indelible impact of some of the most legendary figures in the realm of personal and professional development. This series is a meticulously curated anthology that pays homage to Zig Ziglar, Bob Proctor, Dr. Wayne Dyer, and Jim Rohn—four individuals whose lives and teachings have left an indelible mark on the world.

Mentorship is a timeless concept, a sacred exchange of wisdom, and a guiding light that has illuminated the paths of countless individuals seeking direction, clarity, and purpose. In today's fast-paced and ever-evolving world, the need for authentic leaders and mentors has never been greater. *The Book of Mentors* series emerges as a crucial resource, a compass for those in pursuit of excellence, wisdom, and a life lived in alignment with their highest values.

The celebrity authors, accompanied by the founder and creator, Erik "Mr. Awesome" Swanson and the contributing co-authors in this distinguished series, are an elite assembly of thinkers, leaders, and change-makers. Together, they are creating an everlasting resource of wisdom, intertwining together the legacy of Legacy Legends with the contemporary insights and experiences of today's thought leaders. Their voice, stories, and wisdom are integral roles and lessons as we collectively honor the mentors who have paved the way for us all.

Volume One: Honoring Legacy Legend Zig Ziglar

Zig Ziglar was a master of motivation, a beacon of integrity, and a true champion of the human spirit. His teachings transcended the boundaries of sales and business, touching the hearts and minds of individuals from all walks of life. In the first volume of *The Book of Mentors*, we celebrate Zig's unparalleled ability to inspire action, ignite passion, and instill a deep-seated belief in the potential that resides within each of us. We delve into the core principles that defined Zig's legacy, exploring how his teachings continue to guide, motivate, and transform lives today.

Volume Two: Honoring Legacy Legend Bob Proctor

Bob Proctor was a luminary in the world of personal development, a sage who unraveled the mysteries of the human mind and unlocked the secrets to limitless potential. His teachings on the law of attraction, the power of thought, and the transformative potential of belief have left an indelible mark on the world. In this second volume, we pay tribute to Bob's profound wisdom, delving into the principles that fueled his teachings and exploring the ripple effects of his mentorship across the globe. You will discover a wealth of knowledge, inspiration, and transformation.

Volume Three: Honoring Legacy Legend Dr. Wayne Dyer

Dr. Wayne Dyer was a spiritual guide, a philosopher, and a beacon of light in the journey of self-discovery and spiritual awakening. His teachings on intention, the power of thought, and the connection between the spiritual and the material world have transformed the lives of millions. In this third volume, we honor Wayne's legacy, exploring the depth of his wisdom and the profound impact of his teachings on the world. Just like the *Gifts from Eykis*, here you'll find a sanctuary of wisdom, guiding readers on a journey of inner-exploration, self-realization, and transformative growth.

Volume Four: Honoring Legacy Legend Jim Rohn

Jim Rohn was a philosopher, a mentor, and a visionary in the world of personal development. His teachings on the art of living, the power of personal responsibility, and the importance of continuous learning have shaped the course of mentorship across the globe. In this final volume, we celebrate Jim's timeless wisdom, delving into the principles and practices that defined his teachings. We paint a portrait of a man whose legacy continues to inspire, educate, and elevate the lives of individuals around the world.

The Book of Mentors book series is more than just a collection of books —it is a movement, a legacy, and a testament to the transformative power of mentorship. We are creating a legacy resource that speaks to the heart of what it means to be a mentor, a leader, and a guide in this ever-changing world.

As you turn the pages of each volume, we invite you to immerse yourself in the teachings, the stories, and the wisdom that have shaped the lives of millions. This series is a call to action—a reminder that the journey of mentorship is a lifelong pursuit, a sacred exchange, and a path to transformation. Together, we honor the Legacy Legends, celebrate the mentors who have guided us, and pave the way for the next generation of leaders and changemakers.

The journey begins here, and the path ahead is rich with possibility.

Honoring Jim Rohn

A TRIBUTE TO A LEGACY LEGEND OF WISDOM & SUCCESS

Few names resonate as profoundly in the realm of personal and professional development as Jim Rohn's. Known as a masterful speaker, a compelling mentor, and an architect of transformational change, Jim Rohn's life and teachings continue to inspire millions worldwide. His timeless principles have become a cornerstone for those striving to achieve excellence, lead with integrity, and live with purpose.

This volume of *The Book of Mentors*, created by Erik "Mr. Awesome" Swanson and Integrity Publishing, is dedicated to honoring Jim Rohn, whose legacy shines brightly as a beacon of hope, discipline, and success.

A Tribute to a Legacy Legend: Jim Rohn

Jim Rohn was more than a motivational speaker; he was a philosopher of success whose teachings shaped the lives of countless individuals. With an unparalleled ability to distill complex ideas into simple, actionable steps, Rohn empowered his audiences to think differently, act boldly, and pursue their highest aspirations. Through his lectures, books, and mentorship, Rohn laid the groundwork for a generation of leaders and achievers.

Early Life

Born Emanuel James Rohn on September 17, 1930, in Yakima, Washington, Jim Rohn grew up on a farm, where he learned the value of hard work and self-reliance. Despite humble beginnings, Rohn's life took a transformative turn when he encountered entrepreneur Earl Shoaff in the 1950s. Shoaff's mentorship introduced Rohn to principles of personal development and success that would become the foundation of his career. This pivotal relationship not only changed the trajectory of his life but also set him on a path to inspire millions.

Philosophical Foundations & Key Teachings

At the core of Jim Rohn's teachings were universal truths about discipline, responsibility, and intentionality. He famously stated, "Success is nothing more than a few simple disciplines practiced every day," highlighting the importance of consistent action. His philosophy blended timeless wisdom with practical strategies, offering insights into financial independence, leadership, and personal fulfillment.

Key Teachings:

1. **The Value of Personal Responsibility:** Rohn emphasized that taking responsibility for one's life is the first step toward true freedom and success.

2. **The Seasons of Life:** His metaphorical view of life as seasons taught the importance of preparation, perseverance, and adaptability.

3. **Success Leaves Clues:** By studying successful individuals, anyone can adopt habits and mindsets that lead to achievement.

4. **Work Harder on Yourself:** He urged individuals to focus on self-improvement, believing that personal growth precedes external success.

Significant Contributions & Career Highlights

Jim Rohn's career spanned over four decades, during which he delivered over 6,000 seminars and authored numerous works that continue to influence the field of personal development. His signature program, *The Art of Exceptional Living*, provided a roadmap for achieving balance and prosperity in all areas of life.

Notable Achievements:

- **Influential Speaker:** Rohn's speaking engagements attracted audiences from all walks of life, inspiring business leaders, entrepreneurs, and individuals seeking change.
- **Mentor to Legends:** He directly mentored iconic figures such as Tony Robbins, Les Brown, Chris Widener, Don Hobbs and Darren Hardy, amplifying his impact on future generations.
- **Prolific Author:** Books like *The Five Major Pieces to the Life Puzzle* and *Leading an Inspired Life* remain staples in self-help literature.

Personal Stories & Leadership

Jim Rohn's own life exemplified the principles he taught. He often shared stories of overcoming adversity, such as his early struggles with financial hardship and the lessons he learned from failure. These experiences gave authenticity to his teachings and endeared him to audiences worldwide.

As a leader, Rohn's humility and relatability set him apart. He led by example, demonstrating that success is achievable through disciplined action and a commitment to continuous learning.

Mentorship & Impact on Others

Rohn's mentorship extended beyond personal interactions, as his words reached millions through his seminars, recordings, and written works. He inspired individuals to dream big, set goals, and take actionable steps

toward their visions. His teachings became the catalyst for countless success stories, with many citing Rohn as the turning point in their journeys.

Legacy & Continuing Influence

Jim Rohn's legacy is one of empowerment and transformation. His principles continue to guide individuals toward lives of significance and purpose. The ripple effect of his work is evident in the countless testimonials and tributes from those who have embraced his philosophy.

Foundational Principles:

1. **Discipline Equals Freedom:** Success requires deliberate effort and consistency.

2. **The Power of Association:** Surrounding oneself with positive influences fosters growth.

3. **Invest in Yourself:** Education and self-improvement are lifelong pursuits.

A Literary Legacy: Books That Transformed Lives

Jim Rohn's written works have left an indelible mark on personal development. His books and recorded lectures provide timeless wisdom for navigating life's challenges.

Influential Works:

- *The Seasons of Life:* A metaphorical exploration of life's cycles and their lessons.
- *The Five Major Pieces to the Life Puzzle:* A comprehensive guide to achieving success.
- *The Treasury of Quotes:* A collection of insights distilled into powerful aphorisms.

Celebrating a Life Well Lived

Jim Rohn passed on December 5, 2009, leaving behind a legacy that continues to inspire generations. His life was a testament to the power of ideas, discipline, and mentorship. As we honor his memory, we celebrate not just his achievements but the enduring impact of his teachings on individuals and communities worldwide.

Jim had a huge impact on Erik "Mr. Awesome" Swanson as they shared stages together through the years. Erik attributes the creation of his philosophy of The Habitude Warrior to Jim Rohn when they sat down one day for a chat. Jim had asked Erik a very important question that would direct Erik's success for the rest of his life.

Through his timeless wisdom, Jim Rohn reminds us that greatness is within reach for anyone willing to embrace discipline, seek knowledge, and take bold steps toward their dreams. His legacy is a shining example of a life lived with intention, integrity, and purpose.

~ Habitude Warrior Team ~

ERIK SWANSON

MENTORS COME IN ALL SHAPES & SIZES

"Success is not to be pursued; it is to be attracted by the person you become, and I believe that personal growth leads to success, and that people should improve their skills and mindset in addition to chasing their goals."
~ **Jim Rohn**

The year was 2005, and I had been working with my main Mentor, Brian Tracy, for close to seven years at this point. Working with Brian was such a valuable time in my life. I was a Senior Trainer with Brian Tracy's organization, in which I would travel the world and train not only sales teams of numerous corporations from Fortune 100 all the way down to start ups, but I was also in charge of training, coaching, and managing the vast team of sales trainers that worked for Brian Tracy.

It was such a great experience and brought so much bliss into my life. Was it all fun and games? Absolutely not! Were there grueling times I had to dig deep and find that inner strength to keep moving forward to conquer all of our amazing goals we set up for the company as a whole and all of the team of sales trainers who reported directly to me? Yes!

It was an experience I will never forget and will always cherish. My father would always remind me to seek out greatness. Brian Tracy mentored me directly, and it proved to be one of the best decisions in my life to follow such a master in sales and business development. He truly is one of the all-time greatest motivators in our era.

Brian Tracy has always taught me to seek out those leaders in our field who are changing the world to be a better place. He had always mentioned to me names of self-development gurus from whom I should start learning. Brian was a huge advocate in the habit of learning from the best.

So, I sought out to do exactly that! I wrote all of the names that he suggested I seek out and learn from. You see, Brian never looked at it as any competition. He looked at it as an opportunity for me to learn and grow. I started to call this list of gurus my "Elephant List."

I believe we all should have an elephant list and always be on the lookout to learn from these leaders in our industries. The saying goes, "If you want to go fast, go alone. If you want to go far, go with a team."

Who is on your Elephant List?

Have you started to create a list of leaders in your field who you look up to? I highly encourage you to start that list today. Start writing down a list of leaders who you feel would have a huge impact in your life if you simply started to follow their lead and learn from them.

It's such an astonishing thing when you actually do this. You will start to see that the Universe will open up and start to conspire in your favor. The Universe will tend to put these people directly in front of you in such a way that you may chalk it up to what you may call a coincidence. Trust me, it's not a coincidence. It's the Universe acting in your favor. Embrace this.

Create a Donkey List

Just like you created your Elephant List, you also may want to create what I call a Donkey List. This is a list of individuals who you seem to allow to take up a great amount of your time, yet they mostly bring negative thoughts and experiences to you. It's time for you to take control of this. It's time for you to privately make a list of these individuals and vow to yourself you will not allow them to rent space in your mind anymore.

You know who I'm talking about… those people who you seem to be drained after they unload a ton of negative thoughts and complaints your way. It's time for you to stop hanging around those individuals. All they do is suck the energy right out of you. Enough is enough.

A Pivotal Point in my Life

I was asked to accompany Brian Tracy to a conference in Houston, Texas, with some of our other Sales Trainers. Yes, the year was 2005. Great guess. It was a multi-speaker platform, in which Brian was one of the main keynoters. Excited about the conference, I had always strived to be in the ballroom, learning as much as I could from each of the speakers on the stage.

Brian Tracy was up on stage at this point. All of a sudden, I heard someone calling my name. I looked to my left in the corner of the ballroom and saw a small, statured man who was sitting on one of the chairs. I distinctly remember him having his legs crossed and one of his hands up by his chin as if he were contemplating something.

He said, "Erik, come here. I have a question for you."

I walked over to him, eager to converse with him. I politely said, "Yes sir, what can I do for you?"

He proceeded to ask me, "So, what exactly do you do for Brian Tracy?" Apparently, he had been watching me throughout the conference and knew I was in a leadership role with Brian Tracy's organization.

I replied, "I am one of Brian Tracy's Senior Trainers who travels with him and manages all of the Sales Trainers."

Somehow, he could sense that I absolutely loved working with Brian Tracy, but he also sensed that training salespeople may not be my ultimate calling in life. I have no idea how he could sense this, but just then, he asked me, "So, what do you *REALLY* want to do, Erik?"

WOW! This question really hit home with me. It was not only the question that was so poignant in my life to hear at that moment, but it was also who the question was coming from. You may have already guessed it. The man asking me these questions was the one and only Jim Rohn!

Right then, one of the seminar breaks was announced, and I cordially thanked Mr. Rohn for the question and politely asked if we could resume our conversation after the break.

After much deliberation back and forth in my own mind, I finally knew the answer. I found Mr. Rohn a little while later that day and resumed our conversation. I explained to him, "Mr. Rohn, I have figured it out and I truly appreciate your question to me. I know exactly what I want to do with my life. I want to help myself and people around the world in finding accomplishment and achievements in their daily habits and their attitudes."

Jim Rohn turned to me and said, "Erik, you should put that together!"

So, I did! I'm pretty sure Jim Rohn didn't mean for me to literally put the words together, but that is exactly what I did. I formed and created what is now called "Habitude Warrior." Habitude is a combination of your habits and attitude… *Habitude*!

I have the one and only Jim Rohn to thank for this gift. Through his mentorship and questions, I was able to truly declare my future and the future success of millions who have learned and grown by the Habitude Warrior methods.

Five Pillars of the Habitude Warrior

Over the years, we have developed the five major pillars of the Habitude Warrior method. I'm happy to share them with you below.

- **COURAGE:** One of our Habitude Warrior must-haves is Courage! It is vitally important to walk tall and strong each day, exuding courage and faith in every step you take. People will notice when you show confidence and believe in yourself.

- **PASSION:** One of the best gifts you can give yourself is the gift of passion. Finding your passion is as important as embracing your passion throughout each and every day. People can feel how passionate you truly are about everything you are doing throughout your day and, ultimately, throughout your life.

- **PATIENCE:** To truly be a Habitude Warrior, you must develop the habit of patience. Patience allows you to experience life and all that it has in store for you. Patience allows you to be kind to your fellow human beings and gives you time to hear other people's points of view.

- **STRENGTH:** Life has many aspects, and we all need to have the habit of strength. Strength allows you to get up each and every day to conquer your goals and get through the valleys of life.

- **LEADERSHIP:** Each Habitude Warrior embraces the fact that they are true leaders. Leaders lead from the front. We teach the world how things are done through trial and error. Leaders treat everyone with respect and dignity. Leaders help others grow and realize there is no competition but collaboration.

Become a Mentor

It's time for you to become a Mentor to others. Just like Brian Tracy and Jim Rohn passed their mentorship on to me, I would love to pass my mentorship on to you! With Courage, Passion, Patience, Strength, and Leadership, I would like to gift you with the same gift that was bestowed upon me. I would like to gift to you the present of mentorship, and just like Jim Rohn beautifully said to me way back on that day in 2005, "You should put that together!"

If you would like to be mentored by me personally, simply reach out to us. I will tell my team to be on the lookout for you and your email. Send it to: *Team@HabitudeWarrior.com*

Jim Rohn & Erik Swanson

ERIK SWANSON

As an Award-Winning International Keynote Speaker and Multi-Time #1 International Bestselling Author, Erik "Mr. Awesome" Swanson is in great demand around the world! He speaks to an average of more than one million people per year. Mr. Swanson has the honor to have been invited to speak to many schools around the world including the prestigious Harvard University. He is also a recurring Faculty Member of CEO Space International as well as an Alumni Keynoter at Vistage Executive Coaching. Mr. Swanson is also the recipient of 2024's International Book Impact Award and the United States Presidential Lifetime Achievement Award presented by the White House in 2024 for his ongoing community service and philanthropy work. Erik's speeches can be found on Amazon Prime TV as well as joining the Ted Talk Family with his latest speech called, "A Dose of Awesome."

Erik got his start in the self-development world by mentoring directly under Brian Tracy. Quickly climbing to become the top trainer around the world from a group of over 250 handpicked coaches, Erik started to surround himself with the best of the best and very quickly started to be invited to speak on stages alongside such greats as Jim Rohn, Bob Proctor, Les Brown, Sharon Lechter, Jack Canfield, Lisa Nichols, and Joe Dispenza—just to name a few. Erik has created and developed the super-popular Habitude Warrior Conferences and Speaker Hearts Mastermind & Retreats, which have a two-year waiting list and include 33 top-named speakers from around the world. They are 'Ted Talk' style events which have quickly climbed to the top 10 events not to miss in the United States! He is the creator, founder, and CEO of the Habitude Warrior Mastermind, Global Speakers Mastermind, and Cafe Mastermind. He is also the creator and publisher of many book series such as *The 13 Steps To Riches* book series as well as *The Principles of David & Goliath* book series. His motto is clear: "NDSO!": No Drama – Serve Others!

www.SpeakerErikSwanson.com

DON HOBBS

A MENTOR NAMED JIM

I was eighteen when I first crossed paths with Jim Rohn, a man whose impact on my life would be immeasurable. At that point, I had no idea that our meeting would shape my future, influence my thinking, and ultimately guide me on a path to success I had only dreamed of. Little did I know I was about to embark on a journey of mentorship that would forever alter the course of my life.

I joined Jim's company at eighteen and worked my way up through the sales team to run the Orange County region eventually. By the time I was twenty-four, I had become the President of Jim Rohn Productions. Being around Jim, his programs, and his way of thinking profoundly shaped my life, decisions, and personal development.

During that time, he invested in me through his seminars, leadership training, and private meetings. This exposure transformed my mindset, shaped my values, and influenced my life philosophy. His words still resonate with me weekly in various situations and everyday life.

The Power of Mentorship

Mentorship is not just a relationship; it's a profound force that can guide us like a star in a sea of uncertainty. It provides direction, purpose, and wisdom that can't be found in textbooks or formal education. It's a bond built on trust, respect, and a shared commitment to growth. The transformative power of mentorship is truly inspiring, motivating us to seek guidance and wisdom in our own lives.

HONORING JIM ROHN

The impact of a mentor like Jim Rohn goes beyond mere professional advancement; it touches the essence of who we are and who we aspire to become. It encourages us to push boundaries, challenge norms, and strive for excellence in every aspect of our lives. Through his mentorship, I discovered that true success is not measured by financial accomplishments alone but by the richness of the experiences we create and the legacy we leave behind.

In a world where distractions abound, and the path to success can be elusive, a mentor serves as a compass, helping us navigate the complexities of life. Jim taught me that every challenge is an opportunity in disguise, and every setback is a setup for a comeback. His guidance illuminated my path, showing me that the journey is as important as the destination and that the lessons learned along the way are invaluable, providing a sense of guidance and reassurance in life's complexities.

Mentorship, at its core, is about giving back. It's about sharing the knowledge and insights gained from one's journey to empower others to forge their paths. Jim's influence has inspired me to do just that—to be a mentor, a beacon of light for those seeking direction, and to continue the cycle of growth and transformation that he so generously initiated in my life.

As I continue to walk this path, I am reminded that the true measure of a mentor is not just in their mentees' success stories but in their lasting impact on their hearts and minds. The lessons I learned from Jim are gifts that I carry with me, and they continue to shape my life and the lives of those I have the privilege to mentor. It's a testament to the enduring power of mentorship and the profound connections that can change the world, one person at a time, filling us with hope and optimism for our own journeys.

Jim Rohn was that "guiding star" for me. He wasn't just a mentor but a beacon of light in a world that's ten felt dark and uncertain. His influence didn't stop at the boundaries of a classroom or seminar hall; it permeated my existence. Jim's teachings became a blueprint for my life, and his words continue to echo in my mind, offering guidance in the most unexpected moments.

The Journey Begins

My journey with Jim began when I reluctantly attended one of his seminars at the Westin South Plaza in Costa Mesa, California. I had no grand aspirations or a clear sense of direction then. I went because someone had convinced me to go, and honestly, I didn't want to be there. Little did I know that this moment would become a turning point in my life, a journey that would change my life in ways I could never have imagined.

However, I quickly realized that what I heard was essential for my future. I recognized his influence as crucial to living a more significant life filled with purpose, success, and personal growth. He said, "It's not what happens. What happens happens to everyone. How you respond to it and how your life unfolds as a result makes the difference."

My journey with Jim reveals the transformative power of mentorship. It highlights how a single guiding figure can profoundly influence not just our careers but our entire lives. Under Jim's mentorship, I learned that success is not merely a destination but a continuous journey of growth and self-improvement. His teachings instilled in me the belief that obstacles are opportunities in disguise and that with the right mindset, anything is achievable.

Jim's ability to instill confidence and inspire change was unparalleled. He taught me to see the world through a lens of possibility, encouraging me to embrace challenges as steps to success. His mentorship helped me cultivate resilience and a relentless pursuit of excellence, which have served me well in all my endeavors.

Through my experiences with Jim, I've understood that proper mentorship involves more than just imparting knowledge—it's about empowering others to discover their potential and pursue their dreams. This realization has fueled my passion for mentoring others, hoping to offer them the same transformative guidance Jim provided me.

I am grateful for the wisdom and insights Jim shared. His legacy inspires me to be a better mentor, leader, and person. The lessons I learned under his guidance have become the foundation upon which I've built my life and career. I am committed to paying forward the invaluable gifts of mentorship that Jim so generously gave me.

As Jim stepped onto the stage, he radiated a kind of warmth and authenticity that was instantly captivating. He wasn't just a speaker; he was a storytelling sage and a philosopher all rolled into one. He had an uncanny ability to distill complex ideas into simple, actionable principles that resonated with everyone in the room.

The Gift of Proximity

Jim often said, "You become the five people you are around the most." It's a notion that has remained etched in my heart and mind. What he meant was that our lives are profoundly shaped by the company we keep. We aren't molded and mentored by those we choose to surround ourselves with, whether we know it or not.

Being in proximity to Jim was like being in the orbit of a giant star. His thinking was bigger, his vision broader, and his heart more generous than anyone I had ever met. It wasn't just his words but his way of outing that left an indelible mark. His presence alone was a form of mentorship.

The Jim Rohn Philosophy

Jim had a unique way of distilling life's complexities into simple, memorable aphorisms. One of my favorites was, "It's not what happens. What happens happens to everybody. It's what you do about it that makes the difference in how life works out for you."

This statement encapsulates the essence of resilience and personal responsibility. It was a constant reminder that while we can't control every event in our lives, we can control our reactions. This mindset shift was revolutionary for me, encouraging a proactive approach to life's challenges.

Jim's philosophy emphasized cultivating a positive attitude and taking decisive action. He often spoke about the power of choice, reminding us that every moment presents an opportunity to steer our lives in the direction of our chosen direction. This empowerment was a cornerstone of his teachings, inspiring countless individuals to take charge of their destinies.

Through his mentorship, I learned that setbacks are merely setups for comebacks. Jim's wisdom taught me to view failures not as endpoints but as steps to success. His guidance gave me the courage to embrace risks, learn from mistakes, and continuously strive for personal growth.

In the years since, I've carried this lesson with me, applying it in my professional endeavors and every facet of my life. Jim's influence remains a guiding light, reminding me that our responses, not our circumstances, ultimately define our journey.

These words encapsulated the essence of Jim's teachings. He and wasn't that life's challenges were universal. We all face adversity, setbacks, and unexpected twists and turns. What sets individuals apart is how they respond to these challenges. It's about taking ownership of their life and making choices that lead to growth, "It's using adversity as a stepping stone to success."

The Gift of Jim's Mentorship

Jim didn't just impart knowledge; he instilled in me a set of core values that would guide my decisions and shape my character. His life was a holistic experience, one that transcended the professional realm. It was about becoming a better human being, not just a more successful one.

Jim poured his wisdom into me through seminars, leadership training, and private meetings. He showed me the power of setting goals, personal development, and continuous learning. It didn't teach me the importance of gratitude, the value of hard work, and the significance of giving back.

But beyond the teachings, Jim exemplified these principles in his own life. He wasn't just a mentor in words; he was a mentor in action. He showed me that living a life of purpose and abundance was possible and attainable.

Jim's Ripple Effects & Personal Transformation

Jim often spoke about the ripple effect of our actions. How a single act of kindness, a word of encouragement, or a moment of mentorship could create waves of positive change that extended far beyond what we could see. His own life was a testament to this idea.

As I wasn't on my journey with Jim, I saw the profound impact his mentorship had had on my life. But I also know how that influence has extended to Jimmy's, and I've had the privilege of mentoring. It's a beautiful cycle where the wisdom passed down from one generation of mentors to the next creates a ripple effect of transformation.

A Life Forever Altered

Jim Rohn was not just a mentor; he was a life-altering force. His wisdom, his warmth, and his words continue to guide me on my path, reminding me of the power of mentorship and the significance of the choices we make in life. He taught me that success is not just about achieving external goals but about becoming our best version.

Jim often said, "The greatest reward in becoming a millionaire is not the amount of money you earn. It is the kind of person you must become to become a millionaire." These words encapsulate the essence of his mentorship. It's not just about achieving success but about becoming a valuable person.

As I reflect on the journey I've traveled since that fateful day in Costa Mesa, I am filled with gratitude for the mentorship of Jim Rohn. He was not just a mentor but a beacon of light, a guiding star, and a friend. His legacy lives on in the lives he touched, and I am forever changed because of him.

DON HOBBS

Don Hobbs is the champion of real estate agents, and his work has supported it by enabling agents to live their best lives and own the biggest businesses. He co-founded Expert Partners, a network of Realtors® and elite agents.

Hobbs changed the real estate industry when he co-founded Hobbs/ Herder Advertising, an industry interrupter and leader in real estate agent branding and marketing. His methodology got his clients leading results never seen in real estate before. Creating the most extensive training company in real estate, NAR's Realtor® Magazine named visionary leader Don Hobbs to their "Top 25 Most Influential People in Real Estate."

He has served as the President of SUCCESS Magazine, Executive Vice President of Keller Williams' MAPS, Chairman of the Hobbs Herder Companies, and President of the Jim Rohn Companies.

Don Hobbs has spoken for hundreds of regional, national, and international conferences to over 1.6 million people. Articles about Don have appeared in publications, including Apple News (as the #1 Top Entrepreneur to watch in 2022), SUCCESS magazine, The New York NAR's LA Times, Wall Street Journal, USA Today, Inman News, Apple News, Broker Agent News, and many others.

www.DonHobbs.com

NIURKA

BECOME A TRUE MENTOR

The Essence of Mentorship

Mentorship is more than a surface-level interaction; it's a journey to the depths of one's potential.

Consider the archetypal stories where the mentor plays a pivotal role. Luke Skywalker had Yoda, whose wisdom was, "Do. Or do not. There is no try." Cinderella's transformation was catalyzed by her Fairy Godmother, reminding us that "Even miracles take a little time." Merlin's sage advice guided King Arthur's rise: "This is your moment. Believe in yourself."

In these stories, the mentor is the catalyst for the hero's journey, helping them cross the threshold of their destiny. This is the essence of mentorship—a sacred relationship that empowers the mentee to discover and fulfill their unique destiny.

Beyond Surface-Level Interactions

Mentorship isn't transactional; it's transformational. It's not about merely paying a fee for a service; it's about forming a deep, meaningful connection. A mentor sees their mentee in their entirety, appreciating and nurturing even the parts that the mentee hasn't learned to love yet. This relationship is built on devotion, understanding, and a commitment to the mentee's growth.

Mentors can see beyond the superficial challenges that cloud a mentee's vision. They look past the immediate struggles and see the potential that resides within. By reflecting this potential back to the mentee, mentors help dissolve doubts and fears, encouraging their mentees to rise to the heights of their grand destinies.

Your Unique Path with a Mentor

Whether it leads you to become a "Life Coach" or something else entirely unique to you, your journey begins with mentorship. As the Bhagavad Gita says, "It is better to live your own destiny imperfectly than to live an imitation of somebody else's life with perfection."

The concept of "Imposter Syndrome" has become a buzzword. This is where individuals doubt their abilities and feel like frauds, which often arises when one lacks mentorship. A mentor helps address these feelings by providing the guidance and support needed to develop the confidence and skills necessary for success.

The journey with a mentor is not just about overcoming challenges; it's about discovering and embracing your unique path. A mentor helps you unlock your potential and guides you toward realizing your own unique contribution to the world.

The Mentor's Role in Overcoming Imposter Syndrome

Addressing "Imposter Syndrome" is a critical aspect of the mentor-mentee relationship. This phenomenon often emerges when individuals lack the reassurance and guidance that a seasoned mentor can provide. A mentor helps to unravel these feelings, equipping their mentees with the beliefs and skills essential for their journey. They reinforce that it's not about emulating someone else's path to perfection but about carving out and excelling in one's own unique journey.

Mentors recognize that overcoming such deep-seated doubts is not just about acquiring knowledge but also about internal transformation. They understand that the roots of "Imposter Syndrome" often lie in subconscious beliefs formed in early childhood, and they help their mentees to reframe these beliefs, fostering a mindset of confidence and self-worth.

The Mentor as a Catalyst for Personal Growth

A mentor is more than an advisor or a guide. They are catalysts for profound personal growth and self-discovery. Their role is to help you see beyond your current situation's limitations and envision what could be. They stand with you as you confront challenges, offering wisdom and insight based on their own experiences and learning.

Through the mentorship journey, you are not just learning skills or strategies; you are undergoing a transformation. This process empowers you to align your actions with your highest aspirations, leading to a life that is not just successful but also fulfilling.

The Deep Connection in Mentorship

The connection in a mentorship relationship is profound and heart-centered. A mentor doesn't just see your talents and abilities; they see your fears, your struggles, and your potential. They accept and cherish all parts of you, including those you may have difficulty accepting yourself. This deep, unconditional support is what sets mentorship apart from other forms of guidance.

Mentors provide a mirror that reflects your true self, free from the distortions of fear and doubt. In their presence, you can see yourself more clearly and begin to shed the layers that are not truly you. This clarity is invaluable as you embark on your path to personal and professional fulfillment.

Embarking on Your Mentorship Journey

As you embark on your mentorship journey, remember that the goal is not to become a clone of your mentor but to become the best version of yourself. Your mentor is there to guide you, challenge you, and support you as you discover and pursue your unique path in life.

Whether your destiny is becoming a mentor yourself, a leader in your field, or exploring a path that is entirely your own, the mentorship journey is about unlocking and embracing your unique potential. Your mentor is there to help you navigate this journey, offering insights and perspectives that can only come from someone who has walked the path before you.

On this journey, you will find that mentorship is not just about achieving goals or acquiring skills. It's about personal transformation, about growing into the person you are meant to be. Your mentor will be your ally on this journey, helping you overcome obstacles and see opportunities where you once saw challenges.

The Power of Mentorship

Mentorship is a powerful and transformative journey that can change the course of your life. It's about more than achieving success; it's about discovering your true self and realizing your full potential. With a mentor by your side, you can navigate the complexities of life with greater clarity, confidence, and purpose.

Embrace your mentorship journey with an open heart and an open mind, and you will find that the possibilities are truly limitless. And remember, *when you change, the world around you changes—YOU have that much power!*

NIURKA

NIURKA is the Visionary, Creator, and Leader of Life-Changing, Transformational Events, Courses, Experiences, and Adventures. She is a Transformational Leader and Master Results Coach who has guided hundreds of thousands of people—from all walks of life—to elevate the way they think, speak, and live. Her work inspires, empowers, and guides people to break free from obstacles and create a life of meaning and success... on their terms.

In 2000, she launched her company with the vision of inspiring social transformation through inner evolution. Prior to that, she was the legendary, record-breaking #1 Corporate Trainer, working alongside Anthony Robbins for five years, the world-renowned authority on leadership psychology and peak performance.

Niurka's work unites the business world with essential wisdom from the mind-body-spirit connection. She has been sought out by and has developed customized training programs for many of the finest companies in the world—including Mercedes-Benz, Marriott, Berkshire

Hathaway, Network Marketing Pro, and Anthony Robbins Companies (just to name a few)—who have achieved record-breaking results by applying her strategies.

Niurka's unique blend of linguistics, neuroscience, business mastery, psychology, and spirituality, along with her in-depth understanding of the subconscious mind, creates an integral learning environment that empowers her students to deactivate disempowering mindsets and behaviors, successfully stepping into their unique purpose with power. She is one of the world's leading Master Coaches of NLP (Neuro-Linguistic Programming) and Hypnotherapy, and she has evolved this body of work.

She is also a Master of Time Line Therapy and a Practitioner of Pranic Healing. Niurka has shared the stage with many of the most renowned thought leaders on the planet (see World Class Speaker section below) and is a best-selling author (see Author section below). This wise, intuitive, multicultural, and spiritually centered woman will transfer the power of SUPREME INFLUENCE® to anyone, anywhere. Get ready to QUANTUM LEAP your business, relationships, and life!

She has delivered keynotes for distinguished global audiences, including Success Magazine, Emory University, Luxury Real Estate, Mercedes-Benz, Berkshire Hathaway, Power of Success, The Anthony Robbins Companies, WFG/World Financial Group, Young Living, Network Marketing Pro, The Most Powerful Women in Network Marketing, and many more.

She has shared the stage with many of the finest thought leaders in the world, including Anthony Robbins, Bob Proctor, John Maxwell, Deepak Chopra, John Assaraf, Brian Tracy, Marianne Williamson, Denis Waitley, Phil Town, Brad Lee, and Bill Phillips, just to name a few. To discover more, visit *NiurkaInc.com*.

www.NiurkaInc.com

LARRY NAMER

VISIONARIES & MENTORS: LESSONS FROM A LIFE IN MEDIA

Mentorship stands out as the cornerstone of my growth and success. It's particularly crucial during those early years when you're figuring out your skill set and preparing to step into the world. I've been fortunate to have two significant mentors who shaped me profoundly.

During my early career, while working at Manhattan Cable as an assistant underground splicer, I couldn't quite figure out what to do with my economics degree. It was here that I met Frank Chiaino. He was a man of humble beginnings who rose through the ranks, and he taught me how to navigate the world of working folks. Through his mentorship, I learned invaluable lessons about connecting with people and understanding the intricacies of different roles within an organization.

Later, when Time Incorporated acquired the company, I was introduced to Nick Nicholas, who eventually became the president of Time Warner. Nick's mentorship was pivotal for me in learning corporate discipline.

This combination of guidance—from someone deeply connected to the working class and another entrenched in corporate strategy—made me an unusual entity in Hollywood, where people are often siloed into either finance or creativity. These two mentors taught me how to bridge both worlds effectively.

Early Inspirations & Breakthroughs

Sometimes, success is about being in the right place at the right time. My entry into the cable business began as a temporary job earning $90 a week, crawling under the streets of Manhattan to splice wires. When Time Incorporated took over, they saw potential in a college graduate working underground. Rising through the ranks, I became the Director of Operations for Manhattan Cable at just twenty-five years old.

One of my early inspirations was Jerry Levin. He envisioned taking movies and putting them on satellites to create what we now know as HBO. At the time, we barely understood what satellites were, but his conviction and vision inspired me. Watching him remain steadfast despite skeptics' doubts left a lasting impression on me. It taught me that visionary ideas often live in your gut and can't be explained until they're realized.

This philosophy shaped my approach to leadership. When we launched E! Entertainment, people doubted us. "You're not Rupert Murdoch or Ted Turner," they said. "People don't start global TCV networks; only big media companies can." But Alan Mruvka and I pushed forward, and today, E! reaches 142 countries and has become a massive influence on pop culture.

Our first breakthrough show, *Talk Soup*, was born out of necessity—we had to be creative because no one was handing us large budgets. The show ran for twenty-six years, proving our instincts were spot on.

Learning from Failures

While success is celebrated, failure often holds the most profound lessons. During the early days of the internet, we launched a website, television.com, envisioning something akin to YouTube… ten years too early. We were doing video streaming when technology couldn't support it. Advertisers paid us $25 per 1,000 users while our costs were $5 per

1,000. Then the internet crash hit, and advertisers' rates dropped to 25 cents. Suddenly, more viewers meant more losses.

The experience taught me the importance of understanding the environment—not just where it is but where it's going. Recognizing when to pivot is critical. If I had stubbornly clung to television.com, I wouldn't have gone on to create the number-one TV show in Russia for a decade. Sometimes, letting go opens the door to greater opportunities.

Embracing Technology & AI

Adapting to technological shifts has been a recurring theme in my career. I've been an advocate for artificial intelligence since its inception. When ChatGPT debuted, I dove in headfirst. Tasks that once took me five days —like writing a TV series synopsis—now take an hour. The AI does 90% of the work, and I spend the rest refining. This efficiency lets me focus on what matters—spending time with my grandson, learning new skills, or simply innovating more.

Industries that resist change often lose. Look at how the music industry spent a decade fighting digital music, only to cede control to platforms like iTunes and Spotify. AI isn't something to fear—it's something to leverage. I've even explored AI mentorship through platforms like HISTORA, which lets me query historical figures like Einstein or Shakespeare for guidance. This isn't replacing human mentorship; it's augmenting it in ways we couldn't have imagined.

Modern Mentorship & Representation

Mentorship today isn't limited to face-to-face interactions. I now have access to digital mentors, opening doors for boundless learning. But traditional mentorship—the kind that involves personal relationships— remains vital.

It's why I'm passionate about giving opportunities to unconventional talent. Whether casting a new series or creating a late-night talk show, I aim to break barriers. For example, I'm developing a talk show hosted by Natasha Graziano, a motivational speaker and single mom who went from homelessness to success. She's an inspiration to women under forty, proving that resilience and authenticity resonate deeply.

I'm also inspired by platforms like TikTok and YouTube, which democratize creativity. My latest projects include casting Asian American talent through these platforms and redefining late-night television to make it truly engaging. We don't ask celebrities about their next movie; instead, we showcase new music acts and celebrate untapped potential. Keeping the Wild West of creativity alive is what drives me.

Maximizing Time & Moving Forward

If I could give advice to my younger self, it would be this: Time is finite. Everyone gets the same twenty-four hours, but how you use them makes all the difference. Each night, I self-assess, stripping away ego to evaluate what worked and what didn't. Passion is important, but it's not always enough to sustain you. You need to balance passion with practicality. Recognize when an idea's time has passed and move on to the next.

Mentorship, creativity, resilience—these are the pillars of my career. They've guided me through challenges and triumphs alike. To anyone reading this, know that success is never a straight line. It's a journey filled with lessons, and if you embrace them, you'll find your path, just as I found mine.

LARRY NAMER

Larry Namer is a globally recognized entertainment and media entrepreneur with a career spanning over five decades. Best known as the co-founder of E! Entertainment Television, a groundbreaking network that redefined pop culture, Namer has left an indelible mark on the entertainment industry. Under his leadership, E! grew to reach over 140 countries, launching iconic programs such as *Talk Soup*, *Fashion Police*, and *E! News*, while shaping the careers of numerous pop culture superstars.

Born and raised in Brooklyn, New York, Namer graduated from Abraham Lincoln High School and later earned a degree in economics from Brooklyn College. His career began in the trenches as an assistant cable splicer at Manhattan Cable, where he quickly rose to Director of Operations by the age of twenty five. His entrepreneurial spirit led him to co-found E! Entertainment and subsequently establish multiple media ventures around the world, including Metan Global Entertainment Group, Comspan Communications, and LJN Media.

Namer's ventures have extended beyond the U.S., notably introducing American media to post-Soviet Russia and creating groundbreaking content for Chinese-speaking audiences. His accolades include the President's Award from the National Cable Television Association and the Media Visionary Award from the Kennedy Space Center. Known for his foresight, he has been a pioneer in leveraging technology, such as interactive TV and artificial intelligence, to innovate in entertainment.

Currently, Namer serves as President and CEO of Metan Global Entertainment Group, where he continues to develop new platforms, seek fresh talent, and challenge conventional media boundaries. A true visionary, Namer's legacy is built on mentorship, creativity, and an unwavering commitment to pushing the limits of what's possible in the world of media and entertainment. As chairman of LJN Media, that entity holds Larry's interest in his many ventures both in the US and China (President of Metan Global Entertainment Group).

www.LJNMedia.com

"TIME IS MORE VALUABLE THAN MONEY. YOU CAN GET MORE MONEY, BUT YOU CANNOT GET MORE TIME."

~ JIM ROHN

AMY KEIDERLING

EMBRACING THE PRESENT MOMENT—LIFE IS NOW

As I reflect on my journey and the experiences that have shaped me, I realize that the mentors who have come into my life have been more than just guides—they have been lifelines, anchors, and sources of inspiration in moments of triumph and despair. The power of mentorship is profound; it's not just about receiving advice or direction but about the transformation that occurs when someone truly sees you for who you are and believes in your potential, even when you cannot see it yourself.

My journey with cancer, starting with that first phone call on March 17th, 2020, has been filled with lessons, each one more powerful than the last. However, the most significant lesson I've learned is the importance of living fully in the present moment, and this lesson was solidified through the wisdom of my mentors.

One mentor in particular, Elaine, who urged me to take action with her powerful words, "Life is now," taught me that every moment is a choice —a choice to live, to love, and to embrace the life that is unfolding before us, regardless of the circumstances. She didn't just give me advice; she held up a mirror that reflected my inner strength and resilience. Through her, I learned that life does not wait for us to be ready; it happens in real time, and it's up to us to decide how we respond.

But Elaine wasn't the first mentor to guide me, and she certainly wasn't the last. As I navigated the turbulent waters of cancer, COVID-19, and the challenges that life threw my way, other mentors stepped into my life, each bringing their unique perspective and wisdom. They reminded me that I am not alone, that my struggles are not in vain, and that the power to create the life I desire lies within me.

It wasn't just about battling the disease—it was about transforming my mindset, changing how I viewed my situation, and recognizing that every challenge is an opportunity to grow, learn, and become more than I ever thought possible.

In its truest form, mentorship is about seeing beyond the surface, beyond the immediate obstacles, and into the possibilities that lie within us. My mentors saw potential in me that I couldn't see at the time. They believed in my ability to survive and thrive, pushing me to look at my life from a different perspective. They taught me that my life wasn't just happening to me—it was happening for me.

Through their guidance, I learned to embrace each moment with gratitude, to approach each day with a sense of wonder and curiosity, and to trust in the journey, no matter how uncertain it seemed. I realized that the present moment is all we truly have, and it is in this moment that we have the power to make choices that will shape our future.

As I continue to navigate my road of life, with its twists, turns, and unexpected detours, I carry the lessons my mentors have taught me. I've learned that the most important thing we can do is live fully, embrace the present, and trust that everything we experience is leading us to where we need to be.

My journey isn't over—there will be more phone calls, more challenges, and more moments when I'll need to dig deep and find the strength to keep going. But I know that, with the support of my mentors, the love of my family, and the belief in myself that I have cultivated, I will continue to rise, overcome, and live my life with purpose and passion.

In the end, life is now. It's not something that happens later, when things are perfect or when we feel ready. It's happening right here, right now, amid the chaos, the uncertainty, and the beauty of it all. And it's up to us to seize it, to live it fully, and to become the people we were meant to be.

So, as I move forward, I do so with the knowledge that I am not alone. I am supported by the wisdom of those who have come before me, the love of those who stand beside me, and the strength within me. Life is now, and I choose to live it with all I am.

LIFE IS NOW! LIFE IS NOW! LIFE IS NOW!

AMY KEIDERLING

About Amy Keiderling: Amy Keiderling is a Rebel Soul Guide. She helps to navigate you to find your soul's purpose. Think of her as a co-pilot on the road of life. When the road gets bumpy, curvy, or just seems full of obstacles and detours, we will pull out our Rebel Roadmap and navigate it together.

Amy Keiderling is the owner of Rebel Roadmap, MOdville, as well as an adventure guide with MO Adventures. Amy has always been an avid collector of anything vintage; the instant connection a piece gives you to a memory or story is why she loves her fab finds and creating memories. Amy's passion grew stronger when she met Keith, as his passion for custom vintage cars, motorcycles, and random collectibles grew their collection. When Amy and Keith are not taking adventure lovers on chartered vacations/retreats, or riding around on their motorcycles, you will find them lounging in the middle of MOwhere on their 30-acre Mid-Century Modern Retreat property. LIFE IS NOW! This Amy's battle cry—as she's experienced life from everything from divorce, body image struggles, self-worth, bankruptcy, food stamps, single parenthood, starting four businesses, being a Rock Star Mom and Mimi to her Bigs and Littles, and a cancer warrior fighting Non-Hodgkin's Lymphoma! Amy's road may be "bumpy," but she's grateful for her "off road" adventure called LIFE. Amy encourages everyone to navigate their road of life and follow their inner GPS full of MO Adventures, MO Fun and MO Memories with the ones you love.

Author's Website: *www.ItsAMoAdventure.com & www.RebelRoadmap.com @RebelRoadmap*

Book Series Website: *www.TheBookOfMentors.com*

> *"EITHER YOU RUN THE DAY, OR THE DAY RUNS YOU."*
>
> ~ JIM ROHN

DR. ANGELA HARDEN-MACK, MD

LIVING IN SYNC WITH THE SEASONS

Each day, we are surrounded by nature's rhythms—the steady rise and fall of the sun, the changing hues of the leaves, the blossoming flowers, or the quiet stillness of winter. But living in sync with the seasons is more than just observing these patterns. It's about understanding how these cycles mirror the flow of our lives, offering profound guidance on how to grow, adapt, and thrive.

The seasons teach us that life is not static. It unfolds in phases, each with its own energy, lessons, and opportunities. But too often, we resist these cycles, trying to hold on to summer's warmth when winter arrives, or ignoring spring's call for renewal because we feel stuck in our current routine. Jim Rohn, in his timeless book *The Seasons of Life*, said it best: "Life is about constantly going through a process of beginnings, middles, and endings, just as the seasons of nature do."

By aligning your personal growth, ambitions, and actions with life's natural flow, you tap into an intrinsic harmony that helps you live with greater purpose and fulfillment. Let's explore what each season offers and how they hold the keys to balance and renewal.

Spring: Welcome New Beginnings

Spring blooms with possibility as the earth awakens from its slumber. It is the season of fresh starts, growth, and hope. For farmers, it's the time to prepare the soil and plant seeds, envisioning the crops they will harvest months later. For us, spring can be a metaphor for planting the seeds of our ideas, dreams, and ambitions.

This is the season to dream big, set intentions, and take the first steps toward your goals. Maybe it's starting a new project, forging new relationships, or learning a skill that excites you. Whatever it is, spring reminds us that beginnings are crucial. Without the seeds planted now, there will be no harvest.

But beware of doubt during this time. Often, we hesitate in spring because the results are not immediate. Trust in the process and the potential of your efforts. Spring asks us to show faith in our dreams— even when they're still just seeds in the dirt.

Action Step for Spring:

Take time to reflect on one thing you want to create or pursue. Write it down, break it into small actionable steps, and commit to planting those seeds today.

Summer: Nurture & Work

While summer often brings thoughts of vacations and outdoor adventures, it's also the season that demands the most work. Farmers tend their crops, protect them from pests, and ensure they have enough water and sunlight. The same goes for your goals and aspirations.

It's time to nurture what you began in spring. Show up consistently, refine your processes, and put in the effort required to help your ideas grow. Summer teaches discipline—not the kind that feels forced, but the kind deeply connected to your purpose. Think of it as your time to refine and strengthen what you're building.

Summer also invites us to enjoy moments of abundance in between the work. It's about appreciating the fruits that are beginning to show and celebrating the small wins along the way.

Action Step for Summer:

Identify one habit or routine that will help you nurture your progress. Whether it's waking up an hour earlier to focus on your work or dedicating weekends to self-care, commit to consistent effort.

Autumn: Reap the Rewards

Autumn is the season of harvest. It's when all the hard work of spring and summer begins to pay off. Farmers gather their crops, reaping the rewards of their toil. For us, autumn is a time to pause and celebrate our achievements.

But autumn is also a time of evaluation. Not every seed planted in spring will bear fruit, and that's okay. Failure or unmet expectations during this time aren't signs of defeat but opportunities to learn. They help us refine our approach for the next cycle.

More importantly, autumn reminds us of gratitude. By reflecting on what went right and appreciating how far we've come, we can fully savor the fruits of our labor. This gratitude fuels our vision for the seasons to come.

Action Step for Autumn:

Make a list of your accomplishments and reflect on what worked well. Take a moment to celebrate—whether it's treating yourself to something special or sharing your wins with loved ones.

Winter: Rest, Reflect, & Renew

Winter carries a quiet beauty that encourages reflection. The external world slows down, and the earth takes its time to rest, recharge, and prepare for spring once more. Winter teaches us that rest is not a luxury —it's vital.

Taking time to pause can be uncomfortable. We've grown accustomed to constant activity, associating it with productivity. But winter reminds us that growth happens beneath the surface, even when it looks like nothing is happening. This is the time to look inward, reflect on your year, and recalibrate your priorities.

Winter also reminds us of resilience. Just as the cold, bare trees endure the harshest weather, we, too, carry inner strength through difficult times. It's in this stillness that we often find our greatest clarity.

Action Step for Winter:

Dedicate time to journaling about your year. Reflect on what you've learned, where you've grown, and what you'd like to focus on when spring returns.

Living in Harmony with Life's Seasons

Nature doesn't rush, and yet everything gets accomplished. Seasons change, the earth adapts, and life continues its cycle with grace and rhythm. When we align our lives with these rhythms, we discover a profound sense of balance.

Jim Rohn's wisdom in *The Seasons of Life* reminds us of this cyclical nature beautifully. He said, "Learn how to handle the winters. The winters are those times when life is tough. But without winter, there is no spring. Remember that spring follows winter, and your seasons will come full cycle."

Put simply, every phase in life has a purpose. Each season prepares us for the next, offering its own unique gifts and lessons. By learning to live in sync with the seasons, we stop resisting change and start thriving within it.

Final Thoughts

Whether you're finding yourself in the excitement of spring, the diligence of summer, the rewards of autumn, or the quiet stillness of winter, remember that these are all phases of growth. Each one has a role to play in shaping who you are and where you're headed.

Take a moment to reflect on which season resonates with your life right now. Are there seeds to plant? Goals to nurture? Moments to celebrate? Or rest to prioritize? Wherever you are, honor the season you're in, and trust that it's exactly where you're meant to be.

If you can begin to view life like nature does—cyclical, intentional, and full of opportunity—you'll find that every season holds its own promise of fulfillment, balance, and joy.

DR. ANGELA HARDEN-MACK, MD

About Dr. Angela Harden-Mack, MD: Dr. Angela Harden-Mack, MD, is a trailblazer in holistic wellness, dedicated to empowering busy professional women to reclaim their health, vitality, and work-life harmony. An international speaker, entrepreneur, wellness expert, and ten-time best-selling author, she has been featured in print and broadcast media for her transformative approach blending modern medicine, healing wisdom, and feminine energy.

Author's Website: *www.LiveGreatLives.com*

Book Series Website: www.TheBookOfMentors.com

"YOUR LIFE DOES NOT GET BETTER BY CHANCE, IT GETS BETTER BY CHANGE."

~ JIM ROHN

AZADEH BENNETT

THE COMPOUND EFFECT OF LEADERSHIP IN REAL LIFE

Lessons from Jim Rohn

When I first arrived in the United States, I was searching for direction and inspiration. Everything about my life had changed—the language, the culture, even the way people approached opportunities. As an immigrant from Iran, I carried with me the hope of building a better future, but I also faced the reality of starting from scratch. It was during this time, while working in network marketing that I was introduced to the concept of personal development.

In network marketing, personal growth wasn't just encouraged—it was celebrated. As part of my journey in this field, I began researching personal development online, curious to learn more about what it really meant. That's when I discovered Jim Rohn. From the moment I watched his videos and listened to his teachings, I felt an instant connection. Jim Rohn wasn't just a speaker or a motivator; he was someone who spoke directly to my soul.

One quote in particular became a beacon for me: *"Don't wish it were easier, wish you were better."* Those words were my lifeline when I struggled to adapt to a new culture, pursued multiple degrees at American universities, and faced the uncertainty of finding my path in an unfamiliar world.

Jim Rohn's teachings didn't just inspire me—they empowered me. They reminded me that resilience isn't about avoiding challenges but growing stronger through them. Every time I encountered obstacles, whether it was financial hardship, cultural barriers, or the pressure of building a new identity, I leaned into his wisdom.

His voice became a mentor in my mind, guiding me through the tough days. He wasn't promising an easy road; he was promising a better me, and that was all the encouragement I needed.

Jim Rohn's Core Principles & How They Shaped My Growth

Jim Rohn's teachings were a masterclass in life, delivered with simplicity and wisdom. His ability to distill profound truths into actionable principles made his philosophy feel accessible, even during the most overwhelming times. For me, his core ideas weren't just theories; they became the foundation for my personal and professional growth.

One of his most impactful principles was the *Law of Averages*, the idea that "you are the average of the five people you spend the most time with." This concept opened my eyes to the power of environment and association. It made me reflect on the people I surrounded myself with and how they influenced my mindset, choices, and ambitions. Moving to the United States meant building a new circle, and I became intentional about seeking out those who challenged and inspired me. From mentors in academia to supportive peers in my career, I curated relationships that elevated my growth.

Another guiding principle was Jim Rohn's emphasis on *discipline*. He often said, "Success is nothing more than a few simple disciplines practiced every day." This idea became my mantra as I pursued not one but four master's degrees in subjects as diverse as Marketing, Management Information Systems, Strategic Communication, and Global Studies. Balancing academics and work and adapting to a new culture required unwavering focus and daily effort. Jim's words reminded me that success isn't achieved in giant leaps but in the small, consistent steps we take each day.

Perhaps the principle that resonated most deeply was his philosophy of *taking 100% responsibility for your life*. This idea wasn't new to me—it was the very mindset that fueled my decision to immigrate. But hearing Jim articulate it so clearly gave me a renewed sense of ownership over my journey. No matter the obstacles I faced, from financial struggles to the emotional toll of being away from my family, I learned to embrace responsibility not as a burden but as an opportunity to grow.

Jim also taught me the importance of lifelong learning. His belief that "Formal education will make you a living; self-education will make you a fortune" was a call to action. While formal education gave me credentials, it was the self-education—the books I read, the mentors I followed, and the skills I developed—that truly transformed my life.

Through Jim Rohn's principles, I came to see challenges as stepping stones, not roadblocks. His philosophy wasn't just about achieving external success but becoming a better version of myself. Every lesson was a reminder that the greatest investment I could make was in my own growth, and that has made all the difference.

The Power of Philosophy & Vision

Jim Rohn often said, "Your personal philosophy is the greatest determining factor in how your life works out." This idea of crafting a clear, intentional philosophy for life became a cornerstone for my journey. He taught that success starts with the vision we create for ourselves and is sustained by the philosophy that guides our choices.

For me, this philosophy and vision crystallized in my dream of bringing *Shahnameh's* stories to life through animation. Growing up, these epic tales of Persian culture, heroism, and wisdom instilled in me a sense of pride and belonging. When I discovered Jim Rohn, his teachings gave me the clarity to align this creative dream with my deeper mission: to inspire freedom, unity, and hope in the hearts of people, especially those in Iran.

Crafting a vision isn't enough; it requires action. Jim's teaching that "you cannot change your destination overnight, but you can change your direction" became my guiding light during moments of uncertainty.

Whenever I faced financial struggles or career pivots, I reminded myself to focus on the small, consistent actions that could move me closer to my goals. Whether it was learning new skills in AI animation or writing scripts inspired by *Shahnameh*, I embraced each step as part of the larger journey.

Jim Rohn's emphasis on vision also reinforced the idea that the value of our lives is not measured by what we accumulate but by what we contribute. His wisdom helped me see that my creative projects weren't just about fulfilling a personal dream; they were about preserving a rich cultural legacy and sharing its timeless lessons with the world.

Overcoming Adversity Through Personal Responsibility

Jim Rohn had an uncanny way of turning what could feel like hard truths into empowering calls to action. His reminder to "take full responsibility for your life" gave me strength during my toughest times. When I felt overwhelmed by the challenges of adapting to a new culture, juggling academic demands, or rebuilding after setbacks, I returned to his principle of ownership.

I realized that while I couldn't control external circumstances, I could control how I responded. Each challenge became an opportunity to practice resilience and creativity. For example, when financial struggles threatened to derail my dreams, I focused on what I could do—such as leveraging AI tools to create high-quality content on a tight budget. Jim's teaching that "success is nothing more than a few simple disciplines practiced every day" reminded me to stay consistent, even when progress felt slow.

Mentorship & Leadership

Jim Rohn's legacy as a mentor to millions has always inspired me. He taught that leadership is not about control but about influence—about inspiring others to believe in their own potential. His leadership philosophy mirrors my aspirations to uplift and mentor others, especially women.

As I've grown in my career, I've sought to emulate his example by giving back. Whether through coaching women in leadership, creating empowering content, or teaching others how to use AI for storytelling and business, I've aimed to create a ripple effect of growth and empowerment. Jim's belief in the importance of legacy resonates deeply with me. He often said, "What you become is far more important than what you get." That idea drives me to focus on impact over achievement.

Creating *Shahnameh's* stories as animated films is my way of contributing to something greater than myself—a legacy that celebrates Persian culture inspires unity, and fosters creativity. It's also a way to honor the countless mentors, including Jim Rohn, who have shaped my journey.

Jim taught me that life's greatest rewards come from helping others grow. By living and sharing his teachings, I hope to pass on the torch of mentorship and inspire others to create their own vision, overcome adversity, and lead with purpose.

Actionable Takeaways for Readers

Jim Rohn's teachings are timeless because they are practical and grounded in action. For anyone seeking personal growth, his philosophy offers a roadmap that can be tailored to any life stage or aspiration. Here are some actionable steps inspired by his wisdom that I have applied in my own life:

1. Create a Personal Growth Plan

Success doesn't happen by accident; it requires intentional effort. Start by defining what growth means to you—whether it's advancing in your career, improving relationships, or cultivating new skills. Break down your goals into daily, weekly, and monthly actions. For me, this meant dedicating time to learning AI tools, writing scripts, and mastering storytelling techniques. Consistency is key, as Jim often said: "Discipline is the bridge between goals and accomplishment."

2. Find Mentors & Role Models Who Align with Your Values

The people you surround yourself with influence your mindset and trajectory. Seek out mentors who embody the qualities you aspire to develop. Jim Rohn became a mentor in my life through his books, videos, and speeches. Today, I continue to learn from thought leaders in leadership, creativity, and AI. Remember, mentorship doesn't have to be formal; you can draw inspiration from books, podcasts, or communities of like-minded individuals.

3. Build Resilience & Embrace Change

Change is inevitable, but how you respond to it determines your growth. Jim taught, "It is the set of the sails, not the direction of the wind, that determines which way we will go." Embrace challenges as opportunities to learn and adapt. When I faced setbacks, whether financial struggles or career transitions, I leaned into small, consistent actions to move forward. Resilience isn't about avoiding difficulty— it's about thriving through it.

The Legacy of Jim Rohn in My Life

Jim Rohn's wisdom continues to shape my life in profound ways. His teachings are woven into my daily actions, from how I approach creative projects to how I mentor others. His philosophy of "success is what you attract by the person you become" is a constant reminder that personal growth is the ultimate reward.

Today, I honor his legacy through my work in storytelling and leadership. Whether it's creating animations of *Shahnameh's* stories or helping others leverage AI tools, my goal is to inspire creativity, resilience, and empowerment. His words remind me to focus not just on achieving goals but on becoming a person of value along the way.

I encourage readers to take a moment to reflect on their own mentors. Who has inspired you to think bigger, work harder, and live with greater purpose? Jim Rohn's teachings remind us that the greatest legacies are built not through material success but through the impact we have on others.

As you embark on your own journey of growth, remember these simple yet powerful words from Jim:

"Don't wish it were easier, wish you were better."

AZADEH BENNETT

About Azadeh Bennett: Azadeh Bennett is a creative leader and transformational coach, specializing in harnessing generative AI and creativity to empower individuals and organizations. With a rich background in emotional intelligence, strategic communication, and design thinking, Azadeh helps others unlock their potential and drive meaningful change.

Azadeh's dedication is strengthened by her loving marriage to Jason Bennett, whose unwavering support fuels her passion for transformation and freedom. Together, they exemplify the power of love and partnership in pursuing life's purpose. Armed with master's degrees in MBA, Strategic Communication, and Global Studies, Azadeh blends her knowledge and expertise to guide clients in leveraging their strengths, fostering creativity, and developing innovative solutions to challenges. Her passion for personal and professional growth is evident in every aspect of her work.

Azadeh's vision extends beyond her professional endeavors. She is dedicated to championing freedom and creativity, particularly for women in Iran. Through her work on bringing the mythical epic stories of *Shahnameh* to life using AI and YouTube, she aims to inspire a global audience and remind the people of Iran of their rich heritage and the power of freedom.

A visionary strategist, Azadeh draws inspiration from the world around her. She expresses her creativity through playing the harp, painting, and exploring the possibilities of AI. Her multidisciplinary approach reflects her belief in the transformative power of creativity and innovation.

Author's Website: *www.AzadehBennett.com*

Book Series Website: *www.TheBookOfMentors.com*

"DON'T LET YOUR LEARNING LEAD TO KNOWLEDGE. LET YOUR LEARNING LEAD TO ACTION."

~ JIM ROHN

DR. BETTY SPEAKS

THE POWER OF BELIEF: LEADING THROUGH ADVERSITY

As a Senior Non-Commissioned Officer (NCO), I've had the privilege and responsibility of leading a diverse platoon of forty-five soldiers. Our mission was like many others until we were thrust into a situation that would test not only our skills but also our resolve and belief in ourselves.

The day began like any other, with the usual routine tasks and the camaraderie that often bonds soldiers in the field. However, as the sun climbed higher, we received intelligence of an impending terror attack that threatened our safety and the stability of the region we were tasked to protect. The gravity of the situation quickly set in, and as I looked into the eyes of my soldiers, I could sense the undercurrents of doubt and fear. It was in this moment that the true essence of leadership was called upon.

The Challenge

Leading in such a scenario isn't just about giving orders; it's about instilling confidence in those who follow you, even when the odds are stacked against you. Jim Rohn, a renowned motivational speaker, once said, "Either you run the day or the day runs you." As I stood before my platoon, this quote resonated deeply within me. We were at a crossroads —either we would take control of our destiny, or we would let fear dictate our actions.

The soldiers in my platoon exhibited a remarkable blend of courage and determination. Their resolve to stand their ground, despite the looming threat, was inspiring. However, I could still see the flicker of doubt that lingered, a doubt that could compromise our mission if not addressed. The most critical battle we were facing at that moment wasn't with the enemy outside but with the enemy within—self-doubt.

The Power of Self-Belief

"Let others lead small lives, but not you. Let others argue over small things, but not you. Let others cry over small hurts, but not you. Let others leave their future in someone else's hands, but not you." This quote by Jim Rohn embodies the mindset that I knew we all had to adopt if we were to survive and succeed in our mission. The belief in oneself is not just a nice-to-have in life; it's an essential ingredient for success, especially in life-and-death situations.

As I gathered my soldiers, I shared a story from my past—a time when I was filled with doubt, questioning my capabilities as a leader. I recalled how, as a thirteen-year-old teenager, I often struggled with the idea of who I would become. I wanted to be someone who could be relied upon, someone who others could look up to. Even then, I knew that belief in myself would be crucial. That belief was nurtured by my faith and the guidance of those who saw more in me than I saw in myself.

One scripture that resonated with me during my youth was Philippians 4:13, "I can do all things through Christ who strengthens me." This verse became a cornerstone of my mentality, reinforcing the idea that I was never truly alone in my struggles. It was a source of strength and a reminder that with faith, self-doubt could be overcome.

I also shared another scripture with my platoon, Joshua 1:9, "Be strong and courageous. Do not be afraid; do not be discouraged, for the Lord your God will be with you wherever you go." This verse was not just about spiritual guidance but also about cultivating a mindset of courage and confidence. I reminded my soldiers that while doubt may try to creep in, we must choose to be strong and courageous in the face of adversity.

The soldiers listened intently, and I could see the shift in their demeanor. The fear was still there, but it was no longer paralyzing. It had been replaced by a sense of purpose and resolve. They understood that while we couldn't control the actions of the enemy, we could control our response to the situation. We could choose to believe in our training, in each other, and most importantly, in ourselves.

The Moment of Truth

As the hours passed, the tension in the air was palpable. We had fortified our position and prepared for the worst. Every soldier was at their post, alert and ready. The attack, when it finally came, was as fierce as we had anticipated. But we were ready—not just physically but mentally.

During the cowardly munition explosion, there were moments when the outcome seemed uncertain. The enemy was relentless, and the noise of battle could easily overwhelm the senses. Yet, in those moments, I saw something remarkable. My soldiers, who had once harbored doubt, stood their ground with a level of composure and determination that was nothing short of extraordinary. They moved with precision, communicated effectively, and, most importantly, supported each other with unwavering belief.

As I reflect on being in the midst of the chaos, another quote from Jim Rohn comes to mind: "Discipline is the bridge between goals and accomplishment." The discipline we had instilled in our training, combined with the newfound belief in our capabilities, was the bridge that carried us through that harrowing experience. Each soldier was focused on the goal, not on the fear, not on the doubt, but on accomplishing the mission.

The Aftermath

When the dust settled, we had not only survived the attack but had done so with minimal casualties. The mission was a success, but more than that, we had emerged stronger as a unit. The experience had bonded us in a way that only shared adversity can. The soldiers, who had initially struggled with self-doubt, were now brimming with confidence. They had faced their fears head-on and had come out victorious.

As I debriefed with my platoon, I emphasized the importance of this victory—not just in terms of the mission but in terms of personal growth. I reminded them that the real battle was not fought against the enemy but within themselves. By choosing to believe in their abilities, they had turned the tide in our favor.

Conclusion

In the days that followed, the lessons from that experience continued to resonate with all of us. As a Senior NCO, my role extends beyond just leading in the field; it's about mentoring and developing the next generation of leaders. The events of that day became a cornerstone of my mentoring approach. I often refer to it when guiding young soldiers, especially those struggling with self-doubt.

Jim Rohn wisely said, "You cannot change your destination overnight, but you can change your direction overnight." That day, we changed our direction—not by altering our course but by altering our mindset. We chose belief over doubt, discipline over fear, and as a result, we achieved our goal.

Call to Action

For anyone facing a challenge, whether in the military or in civilian life, I offer this advice: There will always be someone who doubts you, but make sure that person is never you. The power of belief is the greatest weapon in your arsenal. Use it wisely, and there's nothing you cannot overcome.

If you find yourself struggling with self-doubt, consider these resources:

1. *The Power of Positive Thinking* **by Norman Vincent Peale:** This book offers timeless advice on how to cultivate a positive mindset and believe in yourself.

2. **The Bible:** Spiritual guidance can provide strength and encouragement in times of doubt. Verses like Philippians 4:13 and Joshua 1:9 are excellent starting points.

3. **Jim Rohn's Seminars & Books:** Jim Rohn's teachings are a treasure trove of wisdom on personal development and belief in oneself.

Remember, the journey of self-belief is ongoing. Equip yourself with the right mindset, and there is no challenge too great for you to overcome.

DR. BETTY SPEAKS

About Dr. Betty Speaks: Dr. Speaks is a United States Army retiree, the CEO of A Life Change NOW, and Podcast Host of Overcoming Battles by Being Strong and Courageous. The Artist/ Songwriter of the Single *It's A Resurrection*.

She is your Lifetime IMPRINT EMPRESS! She is very passionate about MOTIVATING individuals to resurrect and establish themselves spiritually, personally, or professionally. She's that chosen warrior who inspires others to create A Life Change Now by leaving an INTENTIONAL IMPACTFUL IMPRINT for INFINITY.

Betty is extremely passionate about helping individuals establish themselves and their generational wealth through multiple streams of income and secure their retirement endeavors. She also mentors youthful ladies and other individuals or teams during transformational workshops, one-on-one mentorship, and other total well-being events. Betty Speaks "IT" when she speaks.

Author's Website: *www.BettySpeaks.com*

Book Series Website: *www.TheBookOfMentors.com*

"LEADERSHIP IS THE CHALLENGE TO BE SOMETHING MORE THAN AVERAGE."

~ JIM ROHN

BOPI VILLARINO

THE POWER OF RESPONSIBILITY: MY LESSONS FROM JIM ROHN

I was fortunate to learn at a relatively young age the importance of taking responsibility for my life and the role my mindset plays in shaping my reality. I understood early on that life isn't about playing the victim or waiting for circumstances to change in my favor. The secret lies in a simple yet profound paradigm shift—recognizing that when we take ownership of our thoughts, we regain control over our outcomes.

Over the years, I've found that whenever I've fallen into a poor mindset, the way out has always been through another paradigm shift. It's about being willing to pause, look inward, and challenge the thoughts that are holding me back. This isn't always easy, but it's essential for growth. When we can step back, assess where we are mentally, and choose to realign with a more empowering perspective, we unlock the ability to move forward.

This practice ties directly to my personal motto: "Servant Heart Warrior Spirit." To me, having a servant's heart means being humble, compassionate, and focused on serving others. But having a warrior spirit means having the courage and tenacity to fight through challenges, rise above limiting beliefs, and take responsibility for your growth. Together, they remind me that true strength lies in the balance between kindness and resilience.

Mindset is at the core of this philosophy. It's the lens through which we see the world and ourselves. It determines whether we focus on obstacles or opportunities, whether we give up or persevere, and whether we stagnate or thrive. Jim Rohn's teachings on responsibility and self-improvement reinforced these truths for me, and they continue to guide me every day.

His words, "You cannot change the circumstances, the seasons, or the wind, but you can change yourself," serve as a powerful reminder that our lives are shaped not by what happens to us but by how we choose to respond. With the right mindset and the willingness to embrace personal growth, we can transform any challenge into an opportunity.

Jim Rohn often said, "Don't wish it were easier; wish you were better. Don't wish for fewer problems; wish for more skills. Don't wish for less challenge; wish for more wisdom." These words are a testament to the power of responsibility. They remind us that our success, happiness, and fulfillment are directly tied to our willingness to take ownership of our lives.

Responsibility is not about blame. It's not about taking on guilt for circumstances beyond our control. Rather, it's about recognizing that we have the power to shape our own responses and actions. This shift in perspective is where real freedom begins. When we stop looking for excuses and start looking for solutions, we reclaim our power to grow and succeed.

For me, responsibility has always been a guiding principle. When I'm faced with challenges, I remind myself to focus on what I can control—my attitude, my effort, and my willingness to adapt. This approach not only helps me navigate difficulties but also allows me to seize opportunities for growth.

One of the most profound lessons I've learned from Jim Rohn is the importance of cultivating your mindset as carefully as a gardener tends to their crops. He often said, "Your mind is like a garden. You can plant flowers, or you can let weeds grow." This analogy resonates deeply with me because it captures the ongoing nature of personal growth.

Just like a garden, your mindset requires regular care. If you neglect it, negativity and limiting beliefs can take root and choke out your potential. But if you invest time and energy into nurturing positive thoughts, learning, and self-awareness, your mind becomes a fertile ground for growth and success.

This lesson ties closely to my belief in the importance of paradigm shifts. When I notice that I've fallen into a negative mindset and begin to go down the road of beating myself up, I can recognize this pretty quickly, and I take it as a signal that it's time to reevaluate and make a paradigm shift. I ask myself, "What thoughts am I allowing to take root? Are they serving me, or are they holding me back?"

Jim taught me that it's not enough to think positively; you have to act intentionally. This means feeding your mind with good books, surrounding yourself with uplifting people, and taking steps to align your actions with your goals. When you approach your mindset with the same care and discipline as a gardener, you create the conditions for lasting success.

Jim Rohn famously said, "If you work hard on your job, you can make a living. If you work hard on yourself, you can make a fortune." This principle has been a cornerstone of my journey.

Self-improvement is not a one-time effort; it's a lifelong commitment. It's about recognizing that who you are today is not fixed or final. You always have the ability to grow, learn, and evolve.

For me, self-improvement is deeply tied to being cognizant of my mindset. When I focus on improving myself—whether through learning new skills, seeking out mentors, or practicing self-reflection—I become better equipped to handle challenges and seize opportunities. Personal growth doesn't just benefit you; it allows you to show up as a better leader, friend, and mentor to others.

Jim often said that success is something you attract by the person you become. This idea shifted my focus from chasing external achievements to cultivating internal growth. When you prioritize becoming the best version of yourself, success naturally follows.

One of Jim's most empowering teachings is that discipline is the bridge between goals and achievement. He said, "Success is nothing more than a few simple disciplines practiced every day, while failure is simply a few errors in judgment repeated every day."

Discipline is about consistency, not perfection. It's about showing up for yourself, even on the days when it feels difficult. For me, discipline has been the key to maintaining a positive mindset and staying aligned with my goals. Whether it's sticking to a morning routine, setting aside time for personal development, or practicing gratitude, these small daily habits create momentum.

Jim's lessons on discipline remind me that every action we take is a step in one direction or another. When we choose discipline, we choose growth. And when we build the habit of discipline, we create a foundation of trust in ourselves—a trust that carries us through challenges and fuels our success.

Jim Rohn's teachings have been a source of inspiration and guidance throughout my life. His words remind me that success isn't about luck or circumstances; it's about taking responsibility, cultivating the right mindset, and committing to continual growth.

My journey has been shaped by paradigm shifts—moments when I chose to look inward, challenge my beliefs, and embrace a new perspective. These shifts have taught me that we are never stuck unless we choose to be. We always have the power to change ourselves and, in doing so, change our lives.

As I reflect on Jim's legacy, I'm reminded of the incredible impact we can have on others when we lead with a servant's heart and a warrior spirit. By taking responsibility for our growth and sharing what we've learned, we honor his teachings and inspire others to do the same.

BOPI VILLARINO

About Bopi Villarino: Raised in the picturesque La Costa Carlsbad, California, Bopi, has always been driven by a passion for education and real estate. She holds a Bachelor of Arts Degree in Liberal Studies/Elementary Education from Point Loma Nazarene University. As a dedicated mother to her beloved son Ross Villarino and cherished daughter-in-law Chelsea, Bopi takes pride in her role as a family-oriented individual. Bopi's remarkable journey into the world of real estate commenced at the young age of 18 when she served as a real estate assistant to a top-producing agent. She then ventured into the financial sector, establishing a mortgage company and expanding into the realms of real estate and escrow services.

After fifteen years, Bopi successfully sold their business to a prominent nationwide brand. Bopi continued to soar in her career, assuming pivotal roles such as Vice President of the Western Region for a division of Lending Tree and Managing Partner for a substantial team in the bustling city of Los Angeles. Her versatile skill set encompasses positions such as manager, director of sales, and team lead across various real estate companies, spanning Southern California, Vail, Colorado, and Park City, Utah. Bopi became a certified real estate coach, extending her expertise to business owners and agents throughout the nation. Bopi took the courageous step of resigning from her role as the Utah Principal State Broker, where she oversaw a thriving community of 600+ agents. She founded Distinctive Properties, a real estate company nestled in the scenic beauty of Heber City, Utah. She finds solace and fulfillment in being in nature, and in various activities, including waterskiing, skiing/snowboarding, hiking, SUPing, snowshoeing, and camping.

Author's Website: *www.DistinctivePropertiesUtah.com*

Book Series Website: *www.TheBookOfMentors.com*

DANIEL KILBURN

A LEGACY OF PERSONAL DEVELOPMENT

Jim Rohn is a name synonymous with personal development and motivational speaking. You have probably not heard of his work, just as I didn't for many years—until I finally got the chance to write a chapter about him. I had never followed any of his teachings, so I decided to check out this guy and realized that, even though I wasn't following him, I actually know many of his mentees.

Comparing his influence to that of other bigwigs in the industry would provide you with some idea of his contributions. Rohn's philosophy and teachings have shaped the lives of many, including notable influencers like Tony Robbins, Brian Tracy, and Jack Canfield. This chapter shall discuss Rohn's life, his principles, and how his legacy lives on.

Early Life & Career

Emanuel James Rohn, or simply Jim Rohn, was born on September 17, 1930, in Yakima, Washington. Having been raised in a farming family, Rohn's childhood influences had humbling outcomes regarding his work ethic and how he viewed the world. Shortly after college, he began practicing what he had learned in the business world while still working with the direct sales company Sears.

His life took a sharp turn when he met Earl Shoaff, a successful businessman who became his mentor. This became the spark that ignited

Rohn's passion for personal development. Under Shoaff's influence, principles that later became the cornerstone of his teachings were instilled in Rohn. By the 1960s, Rohn had started lecturing on his insights and had become one of the most in-demand motivational speakers.

Core Philosophy & Teachings

Most of Jim Rohn's teachings are based on a few core principles, which are more about personal responsibility, habits, and continuing to improve yourself. One of the biggest facets of his core teachings is the importance of personal responsibility. I have found this to be a tasty spice in the recipes of success.

A Few of Rohn's Key Ideas:

- **Personal Responsibility:** Rohn had a strong conviction that everyone must take responsibility for their lives. He always said, "You cannot change your destination overnight, but you can change your direction overnight." This idea instills in individuals an obligation to take control over actions and decisions in their lives rather than external circumstances.

- **Habits:** According to Rohn, what one does daily eventually shapes his future. He felt that every small success occurs over time as a result of small regular practice. As he put it, "Success is nothing more than a few simple disciplines practiced every day."

- **Growth & Lifelong Learning:** Rohn urged others to invest in their personal development through reading, attending seminars, and seeking mentorship in order to remain lifelong learners. One of the greatest powers in a person's life is the ability to get an education. Education that starts from within makes all the difference between achieving one's goals and settling for a sufficient living. He once famously stated, "Formal education will make you a living; self-education will make you a fortune."

- **Goal Setting:** Rohn also believed in the principle of setting definite, attainable goals. He thought that goal setting gives a person a sense of direction and purpose to drive toward achievement. He warned, "If you don't design your own life plan, chances are you'll fall into someone else's plan." This reminds me of my three Ps of prosperity: Have a Plan, be Playful, and Persevere. If you do not design your own life plan, chances are you'll fall into someone else's plan. And guess what they have planned for you? Not much.

- **The Seasons of Life:** One of Rohn's unusual similes was the idea of the seasons of life. He likened the various stages of life to the seasons, each with its own set of demands and potential rewards. Recognizing this pattern enables people to be ready for changes and to adjust to them. This is a strong concept here. At some point in our lives, we will have more days behind us than we have in front of us. Start early, fail fast, and learn from our experiences. There are no failures in life, only feedback.

Comparisons to Other Personal Development Gurus

To better appreciate Jim Rohn's impact, comparing his work to other renowned figures in personal development is helpful.

Tony Robbins: Jim Rohn's most popular protege, Tony Robbins, has created an empire of motivational speaking and self-help. While Robbins is known for his high-energy events and practical strategies, Rohn's approach was more philosophical and introspective. Both have a strong focus on mindset and personal responsibility, although they definitely have different delivery styles.

Brian Tracy: Very closely aligned with Jim Rohn's philosophies, Brian Tracy is noted for setting goals, productivity, and personal success. Tracy basically took many of Rohn's ideas, particularly those on never-ending learning and self-discipline, and ran with them. Really, Tracy's books and seminars sound like more structured and systematic versions of Rohn's ideas.

Jack Canfield: The creator of the successful series Chicken Soup for the Soul, Canfield was also greatly influenced by Rohn when it came to the power of positive thinking and setting goals. Canfield's work often uses stories to make a point, rendering it accessible and relatable, much like Rohn's seminars.

Legacy & Influence

The work of Jim Rohn has outlived him by far. His books, such as "The Five Major Pieces to the Life Puzzle" and "My Philosophy for Successful Living," have a positive influence worldwide. Rohn's seminars and audio programs continue to lead in sales records and are hailed as essential tools for personal development. I recommend starting with "The Ultimate Jim Rohn Library."

Rohn's legacy can also be seen in the lives of the hundreds of people he mentored and inspired. Tony Robbins cites him as an early foundational influence on his life and career. Hundreds of successful businessmen and top motivational speakers, such as Darren Hardy and Chris Widener, have cited Rohn as their mentor.

And the wisdom of Rohn stands until today in a fast-paced and ever-changing world. This becomes much more relevant in this age of instant gratification: his principles of personal responsibility, power of habits, and continuous learning. Rohn's teachings remind us of what it really takes to achieve anything: patience, perseverance, and consistency in a world with too much instant gratification.

Practical Application of Rohn's Teachings

Applying the principles that Jim Rohn expounded can lead to dramatic changes in life—be it personal or professional. Here are a few practical ways to imbibe his teachings:

- **Daily Reflection:** At the end of each day, engage in reflection by sitting quietly and thinking about how you carried yourself through the day. Reflect on your action, choice, and approach to getting what you want. The practice breeds personal responsibility and creates continuous improvement.

Form habits in your life that are aligned with your goals and repeat them daily. These habits compound over time and give incredible results.

- **Self-education:** Read books, attend seminars, and search for mentors to guide and support you.

- **Set Clear Goals:** Define your goals clearly and prepare a plan to achieve them. Break down your goals into manageable steps, and set up a timeline accordingly.

- **Embrace Change:** Realize that life has its seasons, so be ready for changes. View challenges as opportunities for growth and learning.

Jim Rohn's works in personal development are invaluable. Many people can trace their lives being transformed and set on a path of success and fulfillment through his philosophy and teachings. By learning and following his guidelines, one can take control of one's life, develop the right habits, and pursue personal growth.

As we reflect on his legacy, it seems clear that Jim Rohn's wisdom will continue to affect and inspire future generations.

DANIEL KILBURN

About Daniel Kilburn: Daniel Kilburn, America's "5-Star Leadership Coach," is a speaker, author, and coach on the topics of Communications, Leadership, Financial Literacy, and Disaster Planning. Daniel will open communications, build resiliency, and develop leadership by preparing you, your family, and your organization to have tough conversations.

Daniel's mission is "Empowering resilience and leadership through proactive communication and disaster preparedness." Put a plan in place and act on it. Dream, Develop, and Deliver.

Daniel is the Urban Disaster Planning Expert with over 30 years of experience training young men and women, foreign nationals, and Department of Defense Civilians to survive on the modern battlefield. His current focus is on Financial Literacy. He is the author of *Family Urban Disaster Planning* and *Commanding Your Future* and co-author of the #1 Bestsellers, *The Book of Influence, a*nd *The Book of Mentors*. He earned his MBA with a minor in Project Management while serving in the U.S. Army as a single father.

Daniel has been featured in *Authority Magazine*, *Lifestyles over 50*, and *WFLA News Channel 8*. In addition to working one-on-one, he teaches live in-person and online events. It is his duty, obligation, and responsibility to tell you the truth.

Author's Website: *www.DanielKilburn.com*

Book Series Website: *www.TheBookOfMentors.com*

"HAPPINESS IS NOT SOMETHING YOU POSTPONE FOR THE FUTURE; IT IS SOMETHING YOU DESIGN FOR THE PRESENT."

~ JIM ROHN

DAWNESE OPENSHAW

TIMELESS WISDOM: THE ENDURING LEGACY OF JIM ROHN

Jim Rohn, a name synonymous with personal development and business acumen, left an indelible mark on the world of mentorship and self-improvement. Today, his teachings continue to resonate with individuals seeking to transform their lives. This chapter pays tribute to Jim Rohn's profound impact as a mentor, exploring his key philosophies and their enduring relevance.

The Power of Philosophy

Jim Rohn's emphasis on cultivating a positive, proactive philosophy is a cornerstone of his teachings. He urged individuals to question their assumptions, challenge their limitations, and adopt a mindset geared towards growth and possibility.

Rohn's own life story is a testament to this philosophy. Born into modest circumstances, he transformed his life through sheer determination and a commitment to personal development. His journey from a struggling farm boy to a renowned motivational speaker and entrepreneur illustrates the transformative power of adopting a success-oriented philosophy.

The Seasons of Life

One of Rohn's most poignant metaphors is the concept of the seasons of life. He likened life's challenges and opportunities to the changing seasons, emphasizing the importance of adapting to each phase. "Learn how to handle the winters," he advised. "They come right after fall with regularity. Some are long, some are short, some are difficult, some are easy, but they always come." This metaphor underscores the inevitability of challenges and the necessity of resilience.

Rohn's wisdom teaches us to embrace the cyclical nature of life. Winters, or tough times, are inevitable, but they are also temporary. Spring follows winter, bringing opportunities for growth and renewal. By preparing for and embracing each season, we can navigate life's ups and downs with grace and confidence.

The Art of Personal Development

At the heart of Rohn's teachings is the art of personal development. He believed that personal growth is the foundation of all success. "Work harder on yourself than you do on your job," he advised.

He championed the idea of setting aside time each day for personal development activities, whether reading a book, journaling, or reflecting on one's goals. Rohn's own daily routine included reading extensively and learning from a diverse array of sources. His commitment to lifelong learning and personal growth serves as an inspiration for anyone seeking to elevate their life.

Rohn viewed personal development not just as a process but truly as an art form. His philosophy imbued this journey with a sense of creativity, individuality, and continuous refinement.

These are ways he considered personal development as a form of art:

1. The Philosophy of Success

"Your philosophy determines whether you will go for the disciplines or continue the errors."

"Success is doing ordinary things extraordinarily well."

Jim Rohn emphasized that personal development begins with a philosophy, a fundamental way of thinking that shapes actions and outcomes. Much like an artist's vision, this philosophy is unique to each individual. Rohn believed that developing a personal philosophy of success requires introspection, critical thinking, and a willingness to change one's mindset. What works for one person may not work for another. He encouraged individuals to experiment and find personalized strategies that resonate with their unique circumstances and goals.

2. Cultivating Creativity & Innovation

"Don't wish it were easier; wish you were better."

Rohn encouraged people to think creatively about their goals and the paths to achieve them. He believed in the power of innovation, urging individuals to find unique solutions to their problems and to approach challenges with a creative mindset.

3. Transformation & Reinvention

"The ultimate reason for setting goals is to entice you to become the person it takes to achieve them."

He viewed personal development as a transformative process. He believed in the power of reinvention, urging individuals to let go of limiting beliefs and habits and continually strive to become a better version of themselves.

4. Inspiration & Influence

"You are the average of the five people you spend the most time with."

Rohn's influence as a mentor extends far beyond his own achievements. He inspired countless others to embark on their personal development journeys, creating a ripple effect of positive influence. This ability to inspire and motivate others is a hallmark of both great art and effective mentorship.

5. Balance & Harmony

"Happiness is not something you postpone for the future; it is something you design for the present."

Rohn emphasized the importance of creating balance and harmony in life. He believed in managing various life domains—work, relationships, health—in a way that supports overall well-being, similar to how an artist balances elements within a composition.

6. Self-Reflection & Introspection

"Discipline is the bridge between goals and accomplishment."

Rohn encouraged individuals to regularly reflect on their lives, assess their progress, and make necessary adjustments. This practice is much like an artist stepping back to evaluate their work and making refinements to enhance its beauty.

His teachings inspire individuals to approach their growth with the same passion, dedication, and creativity that an artist brings to their work. Through his wisdom, personal development becomes not just a means to an end, but a beautiful and enriching journey in itself.

The Power of Goals

Jim Rohn was a strong advocate for goal setting. He believed that having clear, well-defined goals is crucial for success. "If you don't design your own life plan, chances are you'll fall into someone else's plan. And guess what they have planned for you? Not much." This statement encapsulates the essence of Rohn's approach to goals: they are the blueprint for a successful life.

Rohn encouraged individuals to set specific, measurable, achievable, relevant, and time-bound (SMART) goals. He emphasized the importance of writing down goals and creating a detailed plan to achieve them. According to Rohn, the act of setting goals and working towards them instills a sense of purpose and direction, transforming dreams into actionable steps.

Practical Wisdom for Modern Times

While Jim Rohn's teachings are timeless, their application in the modern world is more relevant than ever. In an age of rapid change and uncertainty, Rohn's emphasis on adaptability, resilience, and continuous learning provides a valuable framework for navigating today's challenges.

His advice to "stand guard at the door of your mind" is particularly pertinent in the digital age. With the constant barrage of information and distractions, cultivating mental discipline and focus is essential. Rohn's teachings encourage us to be selective about the information we consume and to prioritize activities that contribute to our growth and well-being.

Influence & Legacy

Jim Rohn's influence extends far beyond his own achievements. As a mentor to countless individuals, including renowned figures like Tony Robbins, he has shaped the lives of millions. His legacy is evident in the numerous testimonials from those who have been inspired and transformed by his teachings.

Many of my personal mentors were mentored by him. So, though I did not have direct personal experience with him, his legacy of mentorship lives on—even through me.

Rohn's impact as a mentor was rooted in his authenticity and generosity. He shared his wisdom freely and encouraged others to do the same. His teachings on mentorship emphasized the importance of giving back and helping others achieve their potential. "We must all suffer one of two things: the pain of discipline or the pain of regret," Rohn often said. This principle not only guided his own life but also inspired others to strive for excellence.

Building a Legacy of Your Own

Jim Rohn's life and work remind us that we all have the potential to leave a lasting legacy. By adopting his principles of disciplined action, personal responsibility, and continuous learning, we can create a positive impact in our own lives and the lives of others.

Rohn's legacy is a testament to the power of mentorship and the ripple effect of positive influence. As we strive to build our own legacies, we can draw inspiration from his example. Whether we are guiding a team, mentoring a colleague, or supporting a family member, we create impact.

Jim Rohn's impact as a mentor and thought leader is a profound testament to the power of personal development and the importance of living with purpose and intention. His teachings offer a roadmap for navigating the complexities of life with wisdom and grace. By embracing his principles, we can transform our lives and create a legacy that reflects our highest aspirations.

Jim Rohn once said, "The ultimate reason for setting goals is to entice you to become the person it takes to achieve them." May we all be enticed to become the best versions of ourselves, inspired by the timeless wisdom of a remarkable mentor whose legacy will forever guide us on our life journey.

Exercises & Reflections:

1. **Philosophy Check:** Reflect on your current life philosophy. How does it align with Jim Rohn's teachings? What changes can you make to cultivate a more positive, growth-oriented mindset?

2. **Seasonal Reflection:** Identify a current challenge (winter) in your life. How can you prepare for the opportunities (spring) that follow? What lessons can you learn from this season?

3. **Goal Setting:** Write down three SMART goals that align with your personal and professional aspirations. Develop a detailed plan to achieve these goals, including daily actions and milestones.

4. **Mentorship Impact:** Consider the mentors who have influenced your life. How have they shaped your journey? What can you do to mentor and support others in your community?

5. **Legacy Building:** Reflect on the legacy you want to leave. What actions can you take today to build that legacy? How can you embody the principles of disciplined action, personal responsibility, and continuous learning in your daily life?

DAWNESE OPENSHAW

About Dawnese Openshaw: Dawnese Openshaw is an agent for CHANGE and is a radically authentic transformational leadership and relationship coach. She is also a John Maxwell certified leadership coach, trainer, and speaker in addition to being a published author in *The Principles of David and Goliath* book series and *The Book of Influence* series and has co-authored a book for adoptive moms.

With over twenty six years of experience in small business and non-profit organizations, in 2020, Dawnese expanded her coaching to include families, which is now her main focus. She teaches emotional intelligence, communication, and relationship building. She combines her passion for leadership and commitment with strengthening families, primarily serving families with teens. Dawnese empowers families to heal individually and together, creating love and harmony in their hearts and homes.

She has been married to her husband, Scott, for twenty eight years, and they are the parents of three amazing children (Randy, Thaniel, and Kayden). They grew their family this summer when Randy got married, adding a beautiful daughter-in-law (Mo).

Author's Website: *www.FullyInvestedFamilies.com*

Book Series Website*: www.TheBookOfMentors.com*

"SUCCESS IS NOTHING MORE THAN A FEW SIMPLE DISCIPLINES PRACTICED EVERY DAY."

~ JIM ROHN

DONNA MINER

THE LIFE & MENTORSHIP OF JIM ROHN

When I think about the pillars of mentorship, personal development and success, Jim Rohn's name definitely comes to mind. Known as one of the foremost philosophers on life and business, Rohn's teachings have impacted millions worldwide. He wasn't just a motivational speaker; he was a mentor to countless individuals, including some of today's most successful entrepreneurs and thought leaders like Tony Robbins and Darren Hardy. However, the most remarkable aspect of Jim Rohn's legacy is the emphasis he placed on mentorship and its profound role in personal growth.

Early Lessons in Mentorship

Jim Rohn's journey to greatness wasn't always a smooth one. Born in 1930 in Yakima, Washington, he grew up on a farm where hard work was a way of life. Despite his humble beginnings, Jim had dreams and aspirations that stretched beyond the farm. His first encounter with the power of mentorship came when he was in his mid-twenties and struggling to make ends meet. Rohn had dropped out of college, was working dead-end jobs, and found himself in debt and uninspired.

Then, he met Earl Shoaff, a successful entrepreneur who would become Jim's first and most influential mentor. Shoaff taught him a principle that would form the foundation of Rohn's teachings: "Work harder on yourself than you do on your job." Rohn quickly realized that if he wanted to change his circumstances, it started with changing himself.

Shoaff's mentorship transformed Jim's life. Shoaff didn't simply hand Jim success, but instead guided him to develop the habits, mindset, and discipline necessary for success. This pivotal relationship ignited a passion in Rohn for personal development, and he began to see the immense value that mentorship can bring.

Mentorship as a Catalyst for Success

For Jim Rohn, mentorship was not just about acquiring knowledge; it was about gaining wisdom. He often said, "You are the average of the five people you spend the most time with." This statement encapsulates his belief that the people we surround ourselves with are instrumental in shaping who we become. Mentors serve as guides who can help us avoid pitfalls, accelerate our progress, and push us to see beyond our limitations. Ask yourself… Who are the five people you spend the most time with? How are those relationships "shaping" you?

Rohn believed that true mentorship wasn't about offering solutions but rather about asking the right questions. A mentor's role, he taught, is to challenge your thinking, open your mind to new possibilities, and hold you accountable to your highest potential.

He used his own life as an example. After learning from Earl Shoaff, Rohn went on to become a millionaire by the age of thirty-one. But even as he became successful, he continued to seek out mentors and surround himself with individuals who could help him grow. This was a lesson he imparted to all his students: "No matter how successful you become, you should always seek mentorship." And he did just that: He was a student for his lifetime.

The Power of Your Story

Jim Rohn had a unique way of connecting with people by making deep concepts relatable. One of his key teachings was that "everyone has a story." He believed each person's experiences—both successes and failures—formed a narrative that could inspire and teach others. I can totally hear his voice in my head as I recollect listening to a recording of him speaking: "It's about your STORY," he would say.

During a seminar, Jim shared how, early in his career, he doubted the significance of his own story. After one seminar, a young man told Jim about his struggles, and Jim could relate. Instead of offering advice, Jim shared his journey—how Shoaff's mentorship helped him grow through personal development. The young man realized that if Jim could change his life, so could he.

I am reminded of something my dad used to tell me. He would say, "You are where you are because you allow yourself to be there." Isn't that the truth!

Jim taught that sharing your story isn't about appearing perfect but about being real and authentic. He reminded people that their story could be exactly what someone else needs to hear to change their life. His philosophy was that everyone's story has value. He believed in the power of genuine stories to inspire, and by sharing his own, he encouraged others to do the same, creating a lasting impact through mentorship and personal growth. This is such an impactful realization and gives us the opportunity to appreciate all aspects and experiences in our lives. I love this.

Jim Rohn's Mentorship Philosophy

Jim Rohn's philosophy on mentorship extended far beyond business and financial success. He believed that mentorship was critical in every aspect of life: relationships, health, personal fulfillment, and spirituality. In one of his seminars, he said, "Success is not to be pursued; it is to be attracted by the person you become." Wowzer! Read that again.

Jim Rohn believed in personal responsibility. He taught that a mentor can offer guidance, but ultimately, it is up to the mentee to act on that guidance. This focus on personal responsibility was a cornerstone of Rohn's teachings. He emphasized that true change begins from within and that while mentors can light the path, it is up to the individual to walk it.

One of Jim's most powerful teachings was that mentorship accelerates the learning process. He likened mentorship to "standing on the shoulders of giants, allowing you to see further than you could on your own." By learning from someone else's mistakes, you save time and energy. More importantly, you gain insights that can take decades to discover on your own. Makes sense, right? Is this what you do, or do you have to learn from you own mistakes? Something to think about.

The Legacy of Jim Rohn's Mentorship

The impact of Jim Rohn's teachings on mentorship can be seen in the success of his mentees. Tony Robbins, perhaps the most well-known mentee of Rohn, often credits Jim for being the catalyst that transformed his life. Robbins met Jim at the age of seventeen, and it was Rohn's mentorship that helped him rise from a janitor to one of the world's most influential motivational speakers. Robbins continues to share the lessons he learned from Rohn, passing on the mentorship philosophy to millions.

Similarly, Darren Hardy, the former publisher of *SUCCESS* magazine, credits Jim Rohn for shaping his career and life. Hardy speaks very often about how Rohn's mentorship taught him the importance of daily discipline, setting long-term goals, and constantly striving for improvement.

Becoming a Mentor, Finding a Mentor

One of the most profound ways to honor Jim Rohn's legacy is by engaging in mentorship, both as a mentor and a mentee. Jim taught that "everyone has something to teach, and everyone has something to learn." If you are in a position to mentor others, you are fulfilling a vital role in helping others grow. On the flip side, if you are looking for mentorship, Rohn encouraged people to seek out those who embody the qualities and success they aspire to achieve.

He believed that mentorship doesn't always have to be formal. You can learn from people through their books, speeches, and even from observing their actions. Mentorship opportunities are limitless, from online courses to podcasts, casual conversations with people who inspire you. The opportunities are everywhere *if* we chose to notice them. What opportunities might you be missing?

Jim's Habits

One BIG thing that sticks out in my mind is that Jim believed in cultivating consistent habits for personal and professional improvement. Here are some key habits he practiced.

1. **Daily Personal Development**: He prioritized personal growth, practicing daily by reading and learning, encouraging at least thirty minutes of study each day.

2. **Journaling**: He kept a journal to record thoughts and lessons, which helped him reflect and track his growth.

3. **Goal Setting**: He mastered specific, measurable goal setting, breaking larger goals into actionable steps and regularly assessing his progress.

4. **Daily Discipline**: He emphasized self-discipline as essential for achieving goals, practicing it in all areas of life through consistent routines and actions.

5. **Time Management**: He valued time as a precious resource, focusing on significant tasks that advanced his goals rather than minor distractions.

6. **Health & Fitness**: He recognized the importance of physical health for energy and clarity, promoting regular exercise and healthy eating.

7. **Mentorship & Association**: He surrounded himself with inspiring people and sought mentors, believing that your circle influences your growth.

8. **Generosity & Giving Back**: He practiced generosity, valuing contributions to others' growth as a measure of true success.

9. **Gratitude & Reflection**: He regularly reflected on his experiences and expressed gratitude, maintaining a positive mindset through appreciation.

10. **Continuous Action**: He advocated for turning knowledge into action, emphasizing consistent, small improvements and calculated risks.

11. **Positive Thinking & Mindset**: He cultivated a constructive mindset, focusing on solutions and viewing setbacks as learning opportunities.

12. **Reflection & Course Correction**: He regularly evaluated his actions and goals, ensuring alignment with his values and avoiding distractions.

These habits centered on personal grown, goal setting, and giving back. Leading him to a fulfilling and successful life. Which of these habits are missing in your life? How different would your life be if you practiced these habits too?

Jim Rohn's life is a testament to the power of mentorship. From his early days with Earl Shoaff to his role as a mentor to some of the greatest minds of our time, Rohn exemplified the idea that success is a team effort, and that mentorship is one of the most powerful tools for growth. His teachings continue to inspire individuals to seek out mentors who challenge them to become their best selves and to, in turn, become mentors for others.

As Jim Rohn said, "If you want to have more, you have to become more." Mentorship is one of the fastest ways to achieve that transformation.

I encourage you to reflect on this: Who in your life has shaped you and had the most significant impact in your life? In what ways can you honor their legacy by mentoring someone else? For me, that influence came from my parents, but that is a story for another time.

DONNA MINER

About Donna Miner: Donna Miner is a seasoned Account Representative with over twenty five years of experience in the real estate industry. Since 1996, she has been a pivotal figure in the sector, showcasing her expertise in sales and her dedication to fostering long-lasting relationships. Donna's passion lies in being an integral part of others' success, taking immense pride in witnessing her clients' personal and professional growth. Her professional journey began at U.S. Title, where she served as a Licensed Escrow Officer in 1996. Donna then transitioned to First American Title Company, where she held dual roles as an Account Executive and Licensed Escrow Officer for over twelve years. Since 2012, Donna has been a Sales Executive at Old Republic Title, located in Clearfield, Utah.

Donna has been the recipient of several prestigious awards, including the Presidents Award by Old Republic Title Central Division in 2022 and the $1,000,000 Producer Award for 2021. Additionally, the Northern Wasatch Board of Realtors honored her with the Presidential Achievement Award in 2021. Earlier in her career, while associated with First American Title Company, she was recognized as the Member of the Year by the Northern Wasatch Women's Council of Realtors in 2011 as well as Affiliate of the Year presented by the Weber-North Davis Board of Realtors in 2004 and 2006. Beyond her professional achievements, Donna is actively involved with committees associated with the Northern Wasatch Board of Realtors as an affiliate and maintains her escrow license. Donna spent many years singing in a band and is now a Sales Representative for a national title company. Her journey has also led her to become a certified Sales Mindset Coach under Jay Shetty's guidance. Her true sanctuaries are found on her patio and the beach, and her most cherished bonds are with her family and close friends.

Book Series Website: *www.TheBookOfMentors.com*

EILEEN E. GALBRAITH

INSPIRE, EMPOWER, SUCCEED

Life is a series of connections and experiences, each offering an opportunity to learn and grow. As women, we often find ourselves juggling multiple roles and responsibilities, feeling the weight of trying to do everything alone. In these moments, the wisdom of mentors, whether met directly or indirectly, becomes invaluable. One such mentor whose teachings have profoundly influenced my journey is Jim Rohn, an esteemed author and personal development speaker.

Jim Rohn's insights into personal development are timeless, providing a framework for understanding and achieving success. His teachings emphasize the importance of nurturing three primary aspects of ourselves: the physical, spiritual, and mental. As a women's coach, I have seen firsthand how these principles can empower women to unlock their potential, achieve their goals, and inspire others along the way.

Decide Who You Are

The journey of personal development begins with self-discovery. Understanding your true self is the foundation for all growth. It's about taking a deep, honest look at who you are, what you value, and what drives you. Here are some questions to guide you in this process:

- **What are my core values and principles?**
- **What are my passions and interests?**
- **What are my strengths and talents?**

- **What areas do I need to improve?**

Answering these questions requires introspection and honesty. It may be helpful to seek feedback from trusted friends or mentors who can offer a different perspective on how they see you. This process can be challenging, but it is crucial for defining who you are and what you want to achieve.

Understanding your true self is the foundation of personal development and success. Take time to reflect on your values, beliefs, strengths, and weaknesses.

Self-awareness allows you to make informed decisions and align your actions with your true self. It involves being honest with yourself, acknowledging your insecurities, and understanding how you relate to others. This process may require deep introspection, feedback from trusted friends or mentors, and a willingness to confront uncomfortable truths. By defining who you are, you set a solid foundation for your goals and aspirations.

Educate Yourself

Once you have a clearer understanding of yourself, the next step is education. Jim Rohn famously said, "Formal education will make you a living; self-education will make you a fortune." Continuous learning is essential for personal and professional growth. Here are some ways to educate yourself:

1. **Read Books:** Exactly what you are doing now: Dive into topics that interest you, challenge your thinking, and provide new insights. Books can be a source of inspiration and a gateway to new ideas.

2. **Attend Workshops & Seminars:** Participate in events that offer learning opportunities and allow you to connect with experts and like-minded individuals. These experiences can provide valuable networking opportunities and practical skills.

3. **Engage in Online Courses & Masterclasses:** The internet is a treasure trove of knowledge. Take advantage of online resources to learn new skills and gain knowledge at your own pace.

4. **Network with Others:** Build relationships with people who inspire you, offer different perspectives, and provide valuable insights. Surround yourself with a supportive and diverse community.

Education is not limited to formal settings. It involves learning from everyday experiences, failures, and successes. Embrace a growth mindset, be curious, and remain open to new ideas and opportunities. Knowledge is power, and the more you know, the more equipped you are to navigate life's challenges.

Inspire Others

As you grow and develop, sharing your knowledge and experiences can be incredibly powerful. By inspiring others, you not only reinforce your own learning but also create a ripple effect that amplifies your impact. Here are some ways to inspire others:

1. **Lead by Example:** Demonstrate the values and behaviors you believe in through your actions. Your integrity and commitment can serve as a powerful example to others.

2. **Share Your Story:** Be open about your challenges, successes, and lessons learned. Your story can resonate with others and provide them with hope and encouragement.

3. **Mentor & Support:** Offer guidance, support, and encouragement to those who seek it. Help others discover their potential and achieve their goals. This could be through formal mentoring relationships or simply being available to listen and provide advice.

4. **Create Impact:** Use your skills and knowledge to make a positive difference in your community or field. This could involve volunteering, starting initiatives, or contributing to causes you care about.

Inspiring others creates a supportive and motivated community. It reinforces your own learning and growth, as teaching others often clarifies and solidifies your understanding. By lifting others up, you also elevate yourself, creating a cycle of positive development and achievement.

Jim Rohn's Principles in Action

Jim Rohn's teachings on the physical, spiritual, and mental aspects of personal development provide a comprehensive framework for success.

1. **The Physical Self:** Taking care of your body is crucial for overall success. Rohn's quote, "You don't do well because you don't feel well," underscores the importance of physical health. Self-care is essential for peak performance. Just as airlines advise you to put on your oxygen mask first before helping others, you must prioritize your well-being to be effective in your roles.

2. **The Spiritual Self:** This aspect involves your beliefs and self-talk, whether positive or negative. It's about understanding that the impossible can become possible with imagination, belief, and action. Your spiritual self is the foundation of your mindset and attitude toward life's challenges.

3. **The Mental Self:** Your self-talk reflects your success. The saying goes, "If you think you can, or if you think you can't, you're right." Read books and seek counsel to nourish your mind. Continuous learning and mental growth are essential for achieving your goals.

Mastering these three aspects guides you toward your desired life. As women, we often teach what we need to learn, gaining self-awareness and guiding others toward their success. I am a prime example of teaching what I needed to learn.

After my divorce in 2000, I filed for bankruptcy and had to educate myself about the U.S. credit system. This traumatic experience led me to build my credit education business and eventually create my coaching business for aspiring women entrepreneurs. I now help them discover who they are and what they want to bring to the world, turning my experience into a privilege of teaching and inspiring others.

Everyone has a purpose, though it might only become apparent through life's circumstances. We get to choose our next steps. Seeking information is powerful when combined with decisiveness, self-belief, and action.

Practical Steps for Personal Achievement

Here are a few steps I believe will guide you on your personal achievement journey:

1. **Self-Reflection:** Answer these questions:

   - How would you describe yourself? Do you love being around people or prefer to observe from the background?

   - Do you let people see the real you, or do you hide behind a mask?

   - Are you competitive, or do you prefer being a silent partner who gets the job done?

   - Can you define what brings you joy, or do you struggle with daily life?

2. **Evaluate Your Responses:** Reflect on your answers:

   - Is this true?

   - How do you know it's true?

   - If it's not true, what is true?

   - What if it wasn't true?

Understanding who you are is crucial for identifying your true desires and figuring out how to achieve them. We are here to support and encourage each other, using our unique talents and skills, which are sharpened through our experiences.

Access to vast amounts of information allows us to learn from diverse perspectives. We can take what makes sense and dismiss what doesn't. Decide the hierarchy of what to act on and achieve success.

Steps to Success:

- **Learn:** Educate yourself through books, workshops, and new people.
- **Refine:** Keep what's useful now and catalog what might be useful later.
- **Decide:** Choose which parts of this knowledge to use and consider the possibilities.
- **Act:** Crystallize your objectives and create actionable steps to achieve them.

As I often say, "Anything is easy when you know how." This belief inspired me to create my Credit Education business, Credit Knowhow.

In Summary:

- Decide who you are.
- Educate yourself.
- Inspire others.

By following these principles, you can create a fulfilling and purposeful life. These steps guide you to achieve your goals, contribute positively to the world, and leave a lasting legacy. As women, we have the power to transform our lives and the lives of others by embracing these teachings and taking decisive action.

EILEEN E. GALBRAITH

About Eileen E Galbraith: Throughout her journey, mentors consistently hailed Eileen's joy in service, her intuitive grasp of people's desires, and her aversion to conventional sales tactics. For Eileen, sales were never about coercion; they were about understanding needs and offering solutions with sincerity and empathy.

However, it was adversity that propelled Eileen into the realm of entrepreneurship. Confronting personal crises, she discovered a reservoir of resilience and empathy within herself, prompting her to extend counsel to other women facing similar challenges. Thus, her accidental foray into entrepreneurship birthed two ventures in the early 2000s, now united under a single banner.

Today, Eileen is not just a sought-after speaker and multi-time Amazon Bestselling author, she is the visionary behind "Implement to Impact," a coaching enterprise dedicated to empowering women entrepreneurs.

With a focus on fostering time freedom, wealth creation, and a supportive community, Eileen's mission resonates deeply with those she serves, embodying the transformative power of empowerment. Learn more about Eileen at: *www.RenewedAbundance.com.*

Author's Website: *www.ImplementToImpact.com*

Book Series Website: *www.TheBookOfMentors.com*

ERIC D. JACKSON

MIND THE MENTORSHIP GAPS

. . . .

Life As A Mentor

"The greatest value in life is not what you get, but what you become."
~ Jim Rohn

I love that our Book of Mentors series started with Zig Ziglar and is completed with honoring Jim Rohn, who was Tony Robbins' mentor when Tony was only age seventeen! As you are leaning into the different facets of mentoring from our authors in this series and the references to the impact of these legends, you might find yourself adding new pieces to your own brand of mentoring and maybe even becoming aware that you sometimes need to "Mind the Mentorship Gaps" that we all experience from time to time.

As Jim Rohn said above, "The greatest value you will receive from life is in who you become because of it," and life and people are not perfect so we must accept the challenge to grow in spite of the obstacles in order to reach the opportunities ahead. That is why "Life as a Mentor" can, at times, be our greatest teacher if we are willing to let it.

Jim Rohn encourages us to learn from life, its principles and its lessons when he encourages us to "work more on yourself than you do on your job or career."

This means you must show up with excellence in your different roles (personally and professionally), but we will also be required in life to work harder on the growth of ourselves in order to experience the fullest potential from life.

"If you work hard on your job, you will make a living. But if you work hard on yourself, you will make a fortune!"
~ Jim Rohn

When you find yourself facing a mentorship gap, do not worry. Remind yourself that "Life is Your Mentor," and at any time you can allow yourself to become more aware, more in tune, and more willing to learn and seek out different forms of learning and new mentors to fill those gaps.

If Jim Rohn were sitting with us right now as you read this, he would likely remind us to stay focused on our lives' fundamentals and priorities in the areas we choose to pursue. He would say we should "major in the major subjects and minor in the minor subjects." He would remind us to focus on the half-dozen areas that will make up 80% of the difference in our success in life and to stay disciplined after it all.

Mr. Rohn would tell us that discipline is the bridge from what isn't yet to what can and will be if we apply our efforts toward achieving worthy goals in each area.

So, what or where are your gaps?

Are there six or so areas of your personal and professional life that you have identified that will almost assuredly guarantee you the successes you define for your life? Are you lacking or missing skill sets in any of these areas?

Perhaps you are somewhat accomplished in most of the areas you have chosen for yourself, but are you open to further growth? Are you committed to a lifelong learning and development of who you are becoming, and how you can level up in each area that is important to you with increasing levels of excellence and distinction, with great character and humanity and service? Jim Rohn would tell us right now that we "must have a plan in each area that matters to you."

Don't take your life, your journey, your success, and your contributions lightly or for granted, thinking that all the magical pieces will just fall into place for you somehow. There will be gaps. There will always be gaps in every area and in every plan.

We all have blind spots. That's why we all need mentors, coaches, and teachers.

We have to realize, no matter how green or how seasoned we are in this development journey, that we are not the end-all, be-all. We cannot do anything worthwhile alone. We cannot accomplish a vision for our life by ourselves when we can barely see the next step or two ahead. And, we aren't even yet the person we need to become yet to take steps three and four of the many more steps that lay ahead.

> *"Success is both a journey and a destination; it is both the steady,*
> *measured progress toward a goal, and the achievement of a goal."*
> ~ Jim Rohn

As you take your personal steps along your journey and the path of your choosing, remember to own your choices, review, reflect, and make adjustments as needed. It is your life.

Realize that there will be directions you hadn't planned on taking, and opportunities in areas you never thought possible. You will regularly hit your own limitations and barriers. And you will grow through each of those to reach the next one. Sometimes, you will feel energized and excited as you make progress. Sometimes, you will feel discouraged and doubt yourself. Do not worry. Do not fear. This is all normal.

You will have different mentors along your journey to help you, to offer unique perspectives and experiences you haven't yet had, and to hopefully help you accelerate from one level to the next better than if you had tried it alone. And when a gap arises, that is okay too. You will learn from life's lessons, and you will find new mentors along the way.

*"Having a strong personal philosophy is the major factor in determining
the success of your life."*
~ Jim Rohn

If you have followed this Book of Mentors series or are about to… then
you will see a theme in each section I have contributed: we can learn
from Crisis, Science, Nature, and Life; we can learn from varied
disciplines, principles, and even the negatives of life just as much, if not
more, as the successes and positives we might find as well.

There are volumes of wisdom from Jim Rohn that I encourage you to
personally study, and I am fairly certain you will benefit in each area that
is important to you by doing so, and you will likely enjoy the time you
spend with him in his material. I do know that Mr. Rohn will encourage
you to grow in your thought processes and your personal philosophies.

A mentor can only help you so far, but when you personally study and
test and prove the principles that work and make them your own in your
application and discipline, then you will create the practices that lead you
to the successes you choose for yourself. You will choose to change your
inputs to get improved outputs. Stay focused on who you want to
become, and overcome those gaps!

*"It's not what happens that determines the major part of your future, the
key is what you do about it—start the process of change, do something
different today—do different things with the same circumstances! We
can't change The circumstances but we can change who we are and what
we do. What you have in the moment you have attracted by the person
you have become—if you will first change, everything will change for
you; to have more, you have to become more! Don't wish it were easier,
wish you were better; don't wish for less problems, wish for more skills."*
~ Jim Rohn

Here are some values you can take into your mentorship opportunities
that will serve you well:

- Accountability
- Humility to Learn

- Responsiveness
- Multiplication

Accountability: I hope this quote by Jim Rohn hits you as it does me, "If your story ever gets into someone else's book or story, make sure they use yours as an **example**, and not a **warning**!"

Humility: This is a good extension of Accountability because we are never always the "example." We have to be continuously aware of when we are repeating patterns of fear or failure, and that means acknowledging we are human and that we make errors. Have your mentors help you see blind spots or areas of self-limitation (or other limitations) so you can correct them as you improve who you are becoming.

Jim Rohn's formula for Fear and Failure is, "A few errors in judgement repeated every day." Are you humble enough to realize you need to look for what you are letting slide every day?

Responsiveness: Jim Rohn said, "If you work on your gifts, they will make room for you." Consider how your responsiveness with your mentors could expand who you are becoming even more if your mindset is to work on your gifts with your mentor so that they make room for the person you are becoming—the person you are meant to be. Open up to possibilities.

Multiplication: The very nature of personal expansion, improvement, and achievement is, by definition, multiplication. Are you taking life's complications and turning them into multiplications of potential and possibility?

More importantly—in my opinion—are you helping others to convert complications into their own multiplications and expansions of who you and they are becoming? Are we raising the bar of excellence, and not leaving anyone where they were before, but offering an opportunity to grow beyond you and themselves?

"To be successful, you don't have to do extraordinary things. You simply have to do ordinary things extraordinarily well."
~ Jim Rohn

"Success is an accomplishment great or small, and it is the understanding of the potential and power of an entire human life; it is an awareness of value, and the cultivation of value through discipline—tangible or intangible; it is a process of turning away from something in order to turn toward something else; it is responding to an invitation to change, to grow, to develop, to become, to move up to a better place with a better vantage point; and mostly, it is making your life what you want it to be. It is not a set of standards from our culture, but rather a collection of personal values clearly defined and ultimately achieved; it is your better life, for you, the design you give it, the dreams you accomplish, making your life be what you want for you—that is success."
~ Jim Rohn

ERIC D. JACKSON

About Eric D. Jackson: Eric Jackson has led high-performance teams for leading organizations in marketing and financial sectors and helped clients from family-owned to Fortune 100 companies achieve their desired results. He is the founder of Transformational Leadership & Culture International, and Jackson Insurance and Financial Services.

As a Champion of People, Leadership and Culture, Eric loves helping people create transformation in what matters most to them, and for their people so they can grow their influence, team, and impact. He helps leaders to GAIN, RETAIN, and TRAIN for high performance results for themselves and for their teams to create breakthrough and take practical action steps toward growth and improvement.

Eric is a certified leadership coach, trainer, and speaker with the Maxwell Leadership Team, and with SCALE Architects and the Predictable Success model. As a speaker, trainer and coach he is also a practitioner in his own life and businesses. He has studied people and leadership since he was in grade school, always driven to find a better way, and to share what he has learned with people so they too can create their own desired life transformations.

In his free time Eric enjoys playing golf, and volunteering with youth leadership programs. Eric is passionate about helping others to make a difference in their lives and the world we live in.

Author's Website: *www.ItsYourLif.com/Books*

Book Series Website: *www.TheBookOfMentors*

FRED MOSKOWITZ

THE IMPACTFUL POWER OF PROXIMITY

Jim Rohn was one of the most iconic and impactful speakers and mentors of his time. Although he passed away in 2009, he continues to make a daily impact on many people around the planet.

As a key figure in the world of self-development, Jim Rohn left us with an amazing body of work full of his teachings, stories, experiences, and witty anecdotes. Thanks to the power of modern technology, this body of work is widely accessible to all. Jim Rohn's lasting presence allows us the unique opportunity to learn and benefit from his teachings through his books, audio and video recordings, and his ideas and shared wisdom, which are passed on by so many of us on a daily basis.

In this chapter, I will share some of my favorite Jim Rohn lessons that have personally impacted me.

The Power of Proximity

One of the most powerful quotes from Jim Rohn that I see shared by so many people is, "We become the average of the five people we spend the most time with."

Have you ever stopped to look at the people you have put yourself around? I invite you to consider this: If you want to make a positive change in your life, a great place to start is by looking at the people you spend most of your time with. What are the qualities that you most admire about them? Are they good role models for you? Are they achieving success in a particular area of life that is calling your attention?

It has been said time and time again that the best way to get to where you want to be is to find other people who are already there and ask for help. Why is that? Because successful people are generally willing to help others.

In life and in business, I have experienced that amazing results can come from collaborations, connections, and relationships. I have found that it is extremely important to spend time each day on building and nurturing your relationships. I make it a daily practice and schedule daily time in my calendar to reach out to people and nurture the relationships I have built over the years. People are genuinely open to hearing from you, especially when you are not calling with an agenda or calling to sell or pitch something to them.

Another interesting observation is that when you spend time around amazing people, you will quickly find that you tend to:

- Have higher-level conversations

- Talk about solving larger problems

- Consume the same content that they do

- Read the books that they read

- Get invited to attend great events that they attend

I have personally experienced the power of this lesson in many ways. Years ago, I reached a point in my life where I really began noticing patterns related to the people I spent time with.

As a computer engineer who worked at many companies in the tech industry, on more than one occasion, I found myself in an unfortunate environment where the company (my employer) was declining in its business cycle and headed on its way to demise. You can imagine the general mood and feelings I was experiencing in the workplace environment—feelings of negativity, blaming, and toxicity.

During one of these downturn periods, I remember going out to lunch with my colleagues, and it was usually quite a somber mood, just like sitting at an outdoor picnic under the cover of dark black clouds. Each time, my colleagues would start conversations that followed similar patterns: one gossiped about the manipulative things that Bob did; another colleague shared about their manager, Sally, who was manipulating results to make one of her team members look bad; and yet another colleague complained about the company's CEO making horrible business decisions while they continued to wine and dine extravagantly on business trips using their company paid expense account.

Even though I was not directly complaining myself, the reality was that simply being present at the table and hearing these conversations around me was having a very negative effect on me.

Outside of the workplace, I was focusing on my personal development and investing in my own education. As a result, I was attending conferences and events, training workshops, and joining masterminds. I was now spending time being in the right rooms with positive growth-minded people.

My associations changed; I was now having uplifting and higher-level conversations and building relationships with amazing people. I was spending more and more time being around people who were playing the game of life at a higher level, and it was having a very positive impact on me. My outlook improved, my mindset was strengthening, and I was experiencing growth.

This dichotomy between two parallel worlds resulted in a strong awareness of the people around me, and I became much more purposeful about the people I spent my time with.

The powerful lesson I learned is that it is better to distance yourself from individuals who fixate on drama or negativity. Place some gentle distance between you and them, and instead prioritize spending time with people who are uplifting and who have a positive influence on you.

> *"Every day, stand guard at the door of your mind."*
> ~ Jim Rohn

Be diligent about the inputs to your mind—the conversations you have (which goes back to the people you surround yourself with), the content you consume, and the books that you read. The idea is to avoid all mental junk food. Junk food may taste good in the short term, but it can be very harmful for us in the long term. This quote from Jim Rohn teaches us that, just like the effect of nutrition on our bodies, we should be mindful of what we feed our minds since what we consistently focus on will affect our thoughts, feelings, emotions, and actions. Our actions are what drive our results.

Have you ever noticed what happens when you watch or listen to the news, particularly the traditional mainstream media outlets? I recently learned of a study that found that in the news, for every one article or coverage item that was about a positive and uplifting story, there were seventeen negative articles or items of negative or 'bad news.'

Why is that? Well, if we take a brief look at the business model for the news media, they want to sell advertising, and advertising spots are valued based on the number of eyeballs that are 'tuned in.' With more viewers watching, this results in higher rates that can be charged for the advertising time. As a side note—one of the most expensive advertising slots is during the Super Bowl, where the average cost in 2022 reached as high as $7 million for a 30-second commercial slot.

Therefore, there is a strong incentive to present news in a way that shocks the viewers, raises their cortisol levels (creating stress), and holds their attention for as long as possible. This benefits the media advertising business model but does not benefit those who consume the news.

Think about all the content that you consume. This includes the films, movies, and videos that you watch, the podcasts that you listen to, the books that you read, and the social media content that you follow. Even music lyrics and marketing messages have a subconscious impact on us. When it comes to the people you listen to, they transmit messages that shape and influence us.

Considering all of this, when we watch or listen to news or any other content, I invite you to take it in with a deeper awareness of your focus. While we cannot control what the media is doing, we can certainly control what we do as individuals and where we direct our focus and attention. This is the heart of Rohn's lesson, which includes the quote, "Every day stand guard at the door of your mind."

> *"Don't wish it was easier, wish you were better! Don't wish for less problems, wish for more skills! Don't wish for less challenge, wish for more wisdom!"*
> ~ Jim Rohn

As someone who works in the investment and financial space, this lesson really hits home for me. Certainly, most of us place a great focus on our financial investing. It is important for building wealth and financial stability.

How about investing in our most powerful asset, which is investing in ourselves? Sometimes, it can be easy to overlook this, which is something that certainly warrants our constant attention and focus.

When we invest in ourselves, we are in the pursuit of constant growth and learning. Nothing is better than having the curiosity and thirst for knowledge of being a lifelong student.

We live in such an exciting time where technology has transformed the availability of information and education. This makes it very easy to find opportunities to invest in yourself to grow and develop your business and personal skills. This can be achieved through attending classes, industry conferences, workshops, seminars, and online trainings. Also, reading (and listening to) books, podcasts, and attending online courses are other great ways to learn. The best part is that we have access to learn from some of the top experts and mentors in every field imaginable.

Each one of us has the ability to overcome any obstacle that stands in our way. By placing attention and intention on developing and growing our skills, we become lifelong learners. It has been said that if we are not growing, we are dying. This emphasizes the idea that growth or decay are the only options. If we stop moving and exercising regularly, the muscles in our bodies begin to shrink. This is known as muscle atrophy.

If you want to grow, to push and challenge yourself, the process becomes very straightforward. Remember that as humans, one of the greatest gifts is that we have free will and dominion. The choice is ours. Get around people who are playing the game of life at a higher level, and watch what problems they are solving and their approach to doing that. And ask for help and counsel from them.

FRED MOSKOWITZ

About Fred Moskowitz: Fred Moskowitz is a Bestselling Author, investment fund manager, and speaker who is on a personal mission to teach people about the power of investing in alternative asset classes, such as real estate and mortgage notes, showing them the way to diversify their capital into investments that are uncorrelated from Wall Street and the stock markets.

Through his body of work, he is teaching investors the strategies to build passive income and cash flow streams designed to flow into their bank accounts. He's a frequent event speaker and contributor to investment podcasts.

Fred is the author of *The Little Green Book of Note Investing: A Practical Guide for Getting Started with Investing in Mortgage Notes* and contributing author in *1Habit To Thrive in a Post-Covid World*.

Author's Website: *www.FredMoskowitz.com*

Book Series Website: *www.TheBookOfMentors.com*

JEFFREY LEVINE

SUCCESS THROUGH THE LENS OF MENTORSHIP

"Success is neither magical nor mysterious. Success is the natural consequence of consistently applying the basic fundamentals."
~ **Jim Rohn**

Throughout my journey, the essence of mentorship has been a compass guiding me toward success. It has revealed paths I couldn't see alone, turned obstacles into opportunities, and transformed fear into faith. With each mentoring relationship, I've discovered that success isn't a solitary endeavor but a collective achievement enriched by shared wisdom.

Mentorship: The Invisible Hand

My first encounter with mentorship came unexpectedly. As a teenager, I was in awe of my next-door neighbor's life. He was a lawyer, exuding confidence and success. When he invited me to join him in court one day, my initial response was no. I didn't see myself in his world. Yet, my inner desire to achieve something greater overcame my hesitation, and I said yes. Watching him in his element sparked something within me—a realization that success was possible if I pursued it with determination.

This neighbor didn't merely invite me to observe; he planted the seed of belief in my potential. His subtle but profound mentorship demonstrated that those who see possibilities beyond our current horizon can significantly influence one's life path.

The Power of Persistence & Faith

Another defining moment of mentorship arose during my public speaking journey. In a Dale Carnegie class, I froze during my first two speech attempts. Overcome with embarrassment, I wanted to quit. But my instructor—a mentor in the truest sense—refused to let me give up. He offered me private coaching, demanding that I have faith in myself and attend every session.

Week by week, I grew more confident, transforming fear into excitement. By the end of the course, I was named the most improved speaker. This experience taught me that mentors provide skills and help you see strength within yourself that you may not recognize.

Learning to Adapt & Thrive

Mentorship often appears in moments of uncertainty. I faced countless rejections when I transitioned from law school to building my career. Applications to prestigious firms went unanswered. Feeling defeated, I sought advice from mentors in my network. They emphasized the importance of relationships over résumés and encouraged me to attend networking events.

Their wisdom was pivotal. At a casual basketball game, a friend mentioned a top financial planning firm vacancy. The following day, I delivered my résumé and landed the job. This was a lesson in adaptation —mentors teach you to navigate life's detours and find success in unexpected places.

The Role of Specialized Knowledge

I stepped into a mentorship role during my father's IRS audit. Drawing on knowledge gained from law school and my advanced tax training, I turned a $20,000 liability into a $2,000 refund for him. This experience solidified my understanding that mentorship isn't just about receiving guidance; it's about sharing expertise to uplift others.

Henry Ford once said he didn't need to know everything as long as he surrounded himself with experts. This philosophy guided my career. I assembled a mastermind group of specialists—attorneys, accountants, and financial planners—to ensure no client problem was insurmountable. These relationships enriched my knowledge and provided clients with unparalleled service.

The Mentorship Mindset & Paradigm Shift

Bob Proctor taught me that paradigms—those mental programs controlling our habitual behavior—can often keep us stuck. I overcame limitations I didn't know existed by reprogramming my subconscious mind. Mentors help identify these blind spots and offer new perspectives.

A pivotal shift happened when I adopted Proctor's "Impression of Increase." By leaving every person feeling empowered, I saw exponential growth in my professional and personal life. This practice, rooted in genuine connection, underscores mentorship's power to transform lives.

Mentorship & the Sixth Sense

Napoleon Hill's concept of the sixth sense, intuitive intelligence, became integral to my mentorship journey. The sixth sense is often communicated through "hunches" or inspirations, helping me navigate life's challenges and opportunities. I recall one such moment vividly. A client faced an overwhelming debt situation, and no analytical solution seemed viable. One morning, during a moment of relaxation, inspiration struck. The solution was unconventional but effective, resolving the client's dilemma and deepening my belief in the power of intuitive thought.

Wayne Dyer's wisdom echoes this philosophy: "When you change the way you look at things, the things you look at change." Mentorship helped me see potential where I once saw problems, proving that the right mindset can transform outcomes.

The Power of Transmutation

In my personal life, I've experienced the transformative power of turning negatives into positives—a principle Napoleon Hill termed "transmutation." At one point, I faced severe burnout from overwork and poor health. A mentor suggested small, incremental changes: focusing on fitness, prioritizing relationships, and embracing mindfulness. These steps not only rejuvenated my life but also enhanced my professional effectiveness.

Small changes compound into significant outcomes. By transmuting challenges into opportunities, I've learned to embrace a mindset of continual growth, a philosophy I strive to instill in those I mentor.

Giving Back: The Ultimate Fulfillment

Later in life, mentorship became my purpose. After selling my business and moving to Arizona, I formed a mastermind group to address personal and professional challenges. From suggesting activities to build friendships to finding new ways to contribute meaningfully, this group enriched my life in ways I hadn't anticipated.

In my financial planning practice, I created opportunities for younger professionals to learn from my experiences. Watching them grow into confident, capable leaders was deeply fulfilling. Mentorship is the ultimate way to leave a legacy, extending your impact beyond your achievements.

Trusting Intuition & Creative Thought

Many of my successes have stemmed from trusting my intuition. Whether solving complex financial problems or making career-defining decisions, intuitive flashes have guided me. For instance, when I faced the daunting task of transitioning my business, a chance encounter led to an offer far beyond my expectations. This "off-the-radar" opportunity underscored the power of maintaining openness and trusting the process.

As Napoleon Hill described, our brains act as receivers of infinite intelligence. By cultivating moments of stillness and reflection, we can access solutions beyond the reach of analytical thought. This principle has been a cornerstone of my mentorship philosophy.

The Mentorship Mindset

If there's one lesson I've learned, it's that mentorship isn't limited to formal relationships. It's a mindset of openness, curiosity, and collaboration. Whether learning from seasoned professionals or guiding aspiring leaders, mentorship creates a cycle of growth that benefits everyone involved.

As Jim Rohn wisely stated, success is the natural consequence of consistently applying the basics. Mentorship is one of those fundamentals—a bridge between potential and achievement. By seeking guidance, offering support, and embracing opportunities to learn and grow, we unlock doors to possibilities we never knew existed.

Mentorship has been the cornerstone of my journey, shaping my career, relationships, and personal fulfillment. It has shown me that success isn't just about achieving goals and lifting others as you climb. As you reflect on your path, consider the mentors who have guided you and the mentees you can inspire. We can create a legacy of growth, learning, and shared success.

Expanding the Legacy of Mentorship

To honor the mentors who have shaped my life, I've committed to expanding their impact by creating platforms for others to thrive. Whether through books, speaking engagements, or mastermind groups, my goal is to amplify the transformative power of mentorship. Investing in others creates a positive effect that extends far beyond our immediate reach, fostering a culture of empowerment and shared success.

This journey isn't just mine; it's a collective endeavor built on the timeless principles of growth, resilience, and mutual upliftment. Through mentorship, we illuminate the paths of others, ensuring the light of wisdom and experience continues to shine brightly for generations to come.

JEFFREY LEVINE

About Jeffrey Levine: Jeffrey is a highly skilled tax planner and business strategist, as well as a published author and sought-after speaker. He's been featured in national magazines, on the cover of *Influential People Magazine*, and is a frequent featured expert on radio, talk shows, and documentaries. Jeffrey attended the prestigious Albany Academy for high school and then went on to the University of Hartford at Connecticut, the University of Mississippi Law School, and Boston University School of Law, and earned an L.L.M. in taxation. His accolades include features in Kiplinger and Family Circle Magazine, as well as a dedicated commentator for Channel 6 and 13 news shows, a contributor for the *Albany Business Review*, and a talk show host for WGY Radio.

Jeffrey has accumulated more than thirty years of experience as a tax attorney and certified financial planner and has given in excess of 500 speeches nationally. Levine is the executive producer and cast member in the documentary *Beyond the Secret: The Awakening*.

Levine's most current work, Consistent Profitable Growth Map, is a step-by-step workbook outlining easy-to-follow steps to convert consistent revenue growth to any business platform.

Author's Website: *www.Strategies.org*

Book Series Website: *www.TheBookOfMentors.com*

JON KOVACH JR.

LEGACY MENTORSHIP STARTS WITHIN

"Work harder on yourself than you do on your job."
~ **Jim Rohn**

Mentorship is a journey of transformation—a partnership that commences with self-reflection and extends into the empowerment of others through relationships. When I ponder over Jim Rohn's enduring advice and his perpetual living legacy, I am reminded that the most influential mentors have dedicated themselves to evolving into the best versions of themselves. As a coach and mastermind leader, I stress this foundational principle: we must foster our own growth before we can uplift others.

Self-mentorship is not just a part but the essence of this philosophy. It's about embracing accountability, nurturing self-love, and committing to daily practices that build resilience and clarity. These practices, such as journaling, meditating, and setting intentions, are rituals that bolster our capacity to lead and inspire others. This is where mentorship truly begins: within ourselves, empowering us to take charge of our growth and inspire others.

Many people believe they are not fixed in their own ways, but on the contrary, their belief systems are unchangeable. Personal development teaches us that we can all change and grow. It's important to be kind to ourselves to attract and surround ourselves with others who uplift us.

Reflecting on whether I am the kind of person I enjoy being around is essential for personal growth. When I genuinely appreciate my own company, personal development becomes a joyful and engaging experience. This transformational journey fosters a deeper love for myself.

If you answer questions dishonestly and find that you're not enjoying your own company, it may indicate that you engage in toxic self-talk and use negative vocabulary with yourself. This lack of love, belief, or faith in your abilities can lead you to become someone who negatively influences and impacts others around you.

To attract high-quality, influential individuals into your life and become someone worth sticking around and spending time with, you must first cultivate a sense of love and trust for yourself. This is where it all begins. Mentorship starts not with others but with yourself.

To receive effective mentorship, you must place yourself in an environment, community, or setting where such mentorship can thrive. This involves reflecting sincerely on whether you are a good person and if you would be someone others enjoy being around. The answers to these questions can lead to significant personal growth and transformation.

If you reverse that question into a manifestation or an affirmation, rather than asking myself the question, "Am I a decent person that people want to hang around?" You can change that into an affirmation such as "I am the kind of person that people love to hang out with." Try thinking and saying it this way, "I'm the kind of person people see as valuable, entertaining, fun, engaging, and important to have in their Rolodex." And it's exciting to say those things to yourself. Not only that, but you should look yourself in the mirror and repeat those daily.

Personal development emphasizes growth, starting from within. By being a good person, you attract others, allowing you to connect with higher-quality individuals. Positive relationships foster growth but be cautious of negative influences that hinder your progress.

Self-aware and emotionally intelligent individuals understand the importance of setting boundaries and knowing when to distance themselves from certain relationships. They are healthy enough to communicate their boundaries clearly and engage in discussions that help resolve differences and misunderstandings. They can also recognize when a relationship isn't right for them and decide to move on if necessary.

Suppose you're somewhere in the middle, and you don't recognize this right away, or you don't see it. In that case, you've got to work on yourself personally and professionally to start seeing the patterns in other people and the types of people you want to surround yourself. Just because somebody is wealthy does not mean you want to hang out with them. That's a terrible reason to want to hang out with someone. You should hang out with people because you have a genuine interest in them, and by hanging out with them, you get so much out of just being in their presence. That's the mutual connection.

Reciprocal conversations arise between individuals who respect each other enough to appreciate the value they gain from their interactions. This dynamic is ongoing; consistently offering your time, talents, resources, and God-given abilities demonstrates that you love and care for someone. This concept is similar across various types of familial, personal, or professional relationships. Ultimately, we categorize these connections differently: business, relationships, wealth, status, community, and more.

So, when taking the steps necessary to surround yourself with the right people and build those relationships and communities, you first need to start loving yourself. The second step is to surround yourself with others who do the same. Like-mindedness follows and attracts like-mindedness. Non-like-mindedness is a deterrent to magnets. There is no attraction.

Don't muddy the waters or cloud the atmosphere with that relationship-seeking if you don't qualify or if you don't put yourself in that position. So, working on yourself as part of self-mentorship is essential before seeking mentorship and community from others.

HONORING JIM ROHN

*"You are the average of the five people you spend
the most time with."*
~ Jim Rohn

Surrounding ourselves with the right people is not just a strategy; it's a necessity. In 2017, I graduated from Utah Valley University, equipped with practical skills such as professional networking, relationship building, and follow-up. However, I was disheartened by the effectiveness of what the world had to offer as a young new graduate. So, I embarked on the journey to construct and cultivate my own networking environment where results-based relationships were inspiring, measured, and proven to last. This was not just a choice but a pivotal step towards my personal and professional growth.

Along came my Champion Circle, an entrepreneur's playground for personal growth, relationship building, and community support. The Champion Circle is a carefully curated group of like-minded individuals committed to personal and professional development. We meet regularly to share our goals, challenges, and successes, and we hold each other accountable to our commitments.

I encourage professionals to focus on personal accountability, audit their inner circles, and ask hard questions: Are these relationships serving their growth? Are they surrounded by people who challenge them to rise higher? It's a community that will make you feel included and supported in your growth journey.

Accountability is paramount. People should hold themselves accountable and create an environment where mutual accountability thrives. Whether through daily check-ins, collaborative projects, or monthly mastermind sessions, the goal is to foster relationships that sharpen one another, just as iron sharpens iron, as Stephen Covey put it in his *7 Habits of Highly Effective People*.

One story that encapsulates this is a member who was hesitant to share their goals during a roundtable discussion. With gentle encouragement and support from the group, they shared their vision and took actionable steps to bring it to life. It was a testament to the power of community—a space where vulnerability becomes a strength and collaboration leads to breakthroughs. I remember feeling inspired by their courage and determination, reinforcing my belief in the power of mentorship and community.

> *"Discipline is the bridge between goals and accomplishment."*
> ~ Jim Rohn

Mentorship without action is like a seed that never finds soil. As Jim Rohn so aptly said, "Discipline transforms dreams into reality." This is a lesson I instill in every mentee: Success is built on the small, consistent actions taken daily. Discipline is the bridge between setting a goal and achieving it. It's about committing yourself and sticking to it, even when it's hard or you don't feel like it. This kind of discipline is what turns dreams into reality. It's a reminder that with discipline, you can turn your dreams into reality.

I like to follow the L.E.A.R.N. framework: **Listen, Engage, Action, Read, Nurture.** This isn't just a mantra; it's a way of life. You are encouraged to set micro-goals each week, whether reading a chapter of an inspiring book, reaching out to a mentor for guidance, or simply reflecting on your progress—these small actions compound over time, creating momentum that drives lasting success.

Champions in all disciplines find ways to L-E-A-R-N every day if they want to be healthy, wealthy, and achieve their goals.

L stands for listening. Take the time to listen to positive audios, such as motivational messages, educational materials, and music that can elevate your mood. I refer to these as positive state changers. Choose anything that helps you get into the right mindset.

E stands for engage. This means connecting with your accountability partners, coaches, and community. Establish positive and consistent communication with anyone who helps you stay focused on your goals.

A stands for action, highlighting the need for daily steps toward your goals. Prioritize your most important tasks; if you save them for later, they may never get done. Focusing on smaller tasks first can leave you drained and unprepared to tackle what truly matters. So, commit to working efficiently on your primary goals.

R stands for reading. Champions in all fields dedicate time to reading, studying, and expanding their knowledge and skills through education, mentorship, and historical examples. I encourage everyone to read daily —whether it's five minutes, five words, or five pages—enough to foster a sense of learning and a desire for more knowledge.

N stands for nurturing, which means you must stimulate your mind, body, and soul. This involves caring for yourself mentally through practices like prayer, meditation, and positive thinking. Nurturing your soul can be achieved through spirituality and other forms of personal growth.

Additionally, it's essential to care for your body by eating healthy, exercising, and engaging in activities that promote learning and development. These are the methodologies I teach and encourage professionals to practice daily. I use these techniques and strategies to help people worldwide.

> *"Only by giving are you able to receive*
> *more than you already have."*
> ~ Jim Rohn

Mentorship involves both giving and receiving. It is a cycle of shared growth that enriches the mentor and the mentee. Jim Rohn emphasized that the legacy we leave behind is measured by our impact on others. As you focus on personal growth and development, your journey will be enhanced by exploring relationships and serving others with love.

My Irrefutable Laws of High Performance and Accountability enhance your success rate and accelerate your achievements and outcomes.

1. Personal Accountability and Integrity
2. Accountability Partners

3. Accountability through Coaching

4. Accountability through Community

Once you have established and effectively integrated the four disciplines into your life, they can significantly assist you in determining what you need to do to achieve your goals. You can set up your life, environment, and relationships for success by creating the necessary disciplines to acquire what you truly desire. Utilizing accountability and adhering to the Irrefutable Laws of High Performance will help you reach your objectives.

I emphasize the importance of having an accountability partner and being specific about your goals. I love referring to Napoleon Hill's *Think and Grow Rich*, which includes the concept of a desire statement. This desire statement requires you to know precisely how much money you want. Additionally, you must be clear about what you are willing to give in return for that amount.

Moreover, it's essential to develop a plan of action and set a specific date for when you aim to accomplish your goal. These elements serve as the blueprint for achieving accelerated success.

I mention this because no book in history has created more millionaires than *Think and Grow Rich*. Instead of searching for other resources, focus on applying the principles in this book and continue cultivating more millionaires as we pursue our objectives.

I teach the importance of setting specific goals, focusing on 90-day Sprint Goals, which last no longer than three months. People can sprint toward short-term goals more effectively than they can engage in long-term pursuits. Individuals can build confidence and repeatedly achieve success by concentrating on achievable yet challenging targets in a short time frame.

Once people realize they can accomplish one task, they can often tackle another. Step by step, inch by inch, you build a foundation, and a few feet can lead to great distances. We believe in the sprint goals methodology, one of the fastest approaches to achieving goals.

A Legacy of Growth & Gratitude

Jim Rohn once said, "Success is neither magical nor mysterious. Success is the natural consequence of consistently applying the basic fundamentals." The journey begins with you—your willingness to grow, to give, and to guide.

Through self-mentorship, purposeful relationships, disciplined action, and a spirit of generosity, we honor Jim Rohn's legacy and the potential within ourselves and others. Let this be your invitation to embark on a mentorship journey that transforms lives—starting with your own.

"Everything you need is already inside you." As I say this quote, I point inward at my heart. You must cultivate the discipline, enthusiasm, and action required to acquire and achieve all you want. As you strive to surround yourself with more significant influences, change your status, and build meaningful relationships, do so with a community committed to changing the world or enhancing your environment. Your surroundings will transform entirely because of who you are, not solely because of the people you surround yourself with. You are the key ingredient in changing your environment and achieving success—no one else can do it.

Some people think they need other people to get better, and while that is true, it starts within. You need to put yourself in rooms with better people because you're a better person, not because they're going to fix you or that they can change you. If you've ever done therapy or gone to therapy sessions, you'll know that everything about those sessions has nothing to do with the fact that the therapist will tell you something, and that one thing will unlock something inside you that wasn't there before. The truth is, it's always been there. You've got everything you need, and everything inside you will help you get where you need to go.

Too many people rely on others to make that change and on others to influence their lives, livelihood, and so much more when, in reality, you are the answer to the change. I love the song by Michael Jackson. The message is beautiful: the man in the mirror is the key to change. We all hold the answer to our growth and personal development. Furthermore, we embody the solution that mentorship requires as the world focuses on growing, building, and providing guidance to many people in the future.

JON KOVACH JR.

About Jon Kovach Jr.: Jon is an award-winning international motivational speaker and global mastermind leader. Jon has helped multi-billion-dollar corporations exceed their annual sales goals, including Coldwell Banker Commercial, Outdoor Retailer Cotopaxi, and the Public Relations Student Society of America. In addition, in his work as an accountability coach and mastermind facilitator, Jon has helped thousands of professionals overcome their challenges and achieve their goals by implementing his accountability strategies and Irrefutable Laws of High Performance. Jon is the Founder and Chairman of Champion Circle, a networking association that combines high-performance-based networking activities and recreational fun to create connection capital and increase prosperity for professionals. Jon is the Mastermind Facilitator and Team Lead of the Habitude Warrior Mastermind and the Global Speakers Mastermind & Masterclass founded by Speaker Erik "Mr. Awesome" Swanson.

Jon speaks on accountability, The Irrefutable Laws of High Performance, and The Power of Mastermind Methodologies. He is a #1 Bestselling Author and a featured keynote on SpeakUp TV, an Amazon Prime TV series, with his keynote speech titled, *Getting Unstuck*. In addition, he stars in over 100 speaking stages, podcasts, and live international summits each year. Jon's motivational messages have been viewed by over 300,000 people online. His voice has been used by global brands and creators on TikTok and Instagram Reels, such as: Red Bull USA, Michael Bublé, The NHL, Powell Books, GoDaddy Studio, Canada's Wonderland Amusement Park, and the LSU Cheer Team.

Author's website: *www.SpeakerJonKovachJr.com*
Book Series Website: *www.TheBookOfMentors.com*

"DON'T WISH IT WAS EASIER, WISH YOU WERE BETTER."

~ JIM ROHN

JULIE DELGADILLO

SELF MENTORSHIP & RECIPROCAL EMPOWERMENT

Mentorship has always been an anchor of mine. More than just guidance, mentoring is an experience that transforms both mentor and mentee in equal measure. In previous chapters in this series, I've shared how mentoring has guided my life—from the early days when I learned leadership through my parents' influence to pivotal moments when mentors such as Miss Hazel and Barbara helped me realize my potential.

What happens, then, once one has received mentorship and all that wisdom and support? How do we apply it in life and pass it along? Now, I find myself at an impasse where mentorship becomes something I embody rather than something to seek.

Mentorship as a Mutual Relationship

I have realized that mentorship is not a linear path—instead, it is more cyclical; giving and receiving are interwoven in their existence. Mentors have played an instrumental role in shaping my path while learning something valuable from me. Mentorship's powerful legacy lies within this reciprocity: its essence rests within its ability to recognize that, although people seek guidance, they also bring something of their own to offer in return.

Unknowingly, I found myself serving as an unwitting mentor. It happened unexpectedly during one of those everyday interactions you might take for granted: A young woman in my community approached me asking for advice on balancing work and personal life. She admired my work while telling me she admired me as someone who had it all together despite her struggles. This realization was full circle for me when I realized that those challenges I had overcome could serve as roadmaps to others needing advice and mentorship.

Mentorship isn't about having all the answers; instead, it is about sharing our journey, lessons, and vulnerabilities—walking alongside someone while they navigate their path with support when necessary, offering assistance when they stumble, or celebrating their victories as though they were your own! I was lucky to become friends with this young lady as she and I became mentor-mentee relationships—her unique perspective inspired me to keep pushing through even when the going got tough!

Mentorship is an evolving concept. My consideration of my mentors has allowed me to witness an evolution in how I view and approach mentorship. At first, mentors provided resources, and knowledge gaps were filled by providing tools like Miss Hazel (described in previous chapter contributions). She helped me navigate academic challenges while instilling confidence and resilience, which served me through an extremely transformative period by showing my potential and aligning me with my purpose.

Now, I find myself at another stage of mentorship, one where the boundaries between mentor and mentee blur more fluidly than ever. Mentorship doesn't just involve learning from more experienced people; rather, it should include taking advantage of all possible sources of wisdom if we allow it. Everyone you come into contact with has something valuable to impart if only we listen.

Mentorship is a collaborative experience. I no longer view it as something for which I need an external instructor as much as something I seek internally through peers and colleagues, including friends, mentees, or anyone who may seem unrelated. Some of my most influential mentors may even remain unaware that they're mentoring me; friends, colleagues or even my mentees provide challenges, push my comfort zone away and illuminate parts of myself that I may have otherwise failed to recognize fully.

Mentorship as an Agent of Change

Empowerment has always been at the core of my work, and mentorship plays a central role. Mentorship doesn't provide new power but reveals their existing power for greater independence. I strive to foster strengths by nurturing them to help discover potential within them while offering the support necessary to navigate any potential roadblocks they might come up against in life.

One of the greatest joys of mentoring others is witnessing their transformations. I have had the honor of mentoring many women and young people over time, and the greatest moments have come when they begin seeing themselves as I see them: capable, strong, and full of potential. Mentorship should not involve forcing someone into being someone they aren't; rather, it should assist individuals in becoming their very best selves.

Maria came to me feeling uncertain about herself and her career path yet lacking the confidence to step into them powerfully. Through our conversations and the challenges I offered her, over time, Maria began seeing herself differently, taking risks more frequently, speaking up more, and taking up opportunities she previously avoided. Watching Maria transform into an empowered leader is truly one of my life's most satisfying experiences!

Maria's journey taught me an invaluable lesson about patience in mentorship. Personal and professional growth does not occur overnight; it requires hard work, dedication, encouragement, and persistence from everyone involved. Mentors must remain patient while giving our mentees the space they need to develop, remembering that our role as supporters should not include pushing.

Self-Mentorship is Essential

As much as I appreciate having mentors, one of the greatest sources of guidance and strength can come from within yourself. Self-mentorship involves applying lessons you've learned from others into your everyday life while becoming your biggest cheerleader, guide, and source of strength.

As I matured, I became less dependent on external mentors to guide me. Now that I trust myself more and listen to myself more closely, I seek guidance within myself more frequently rather than externally. That doesn't mean I no longer seek mentorship from others—quite the opposite, in fact—but rather that I know how to balance external guidance with internal wisdom.

Reflection has become one of my primary forms of self-mentorship, helping to keep me grounded and focused even when the road ahead may not always seem clear. I take time every week to reflect upon past experiences, examine lessons learned, and decide how they might apply in my everyday life moving forward. This practice has proven essential in staying grounded and focused no matter the obstacles.

Self-compassion is another critical aspect of self-mentorship that I found indispensable. Recognizing your humanity and realizing you will make mistakes is essential to treating yourself with the kindness and understanding you would show a mentee. Self-compassion has proven invaluable in helping me face life's obstacles with grace and resilience.

Mentorship isn't something to graduate from—it evolves with your life stages. My focus as a mentor lies in supporting others to become mentors while continuing my growth by finding opportunities to learn from others, challenge assumptions, and expand my understanding of what it means to mentor someone else. Successful mentors remain open-minded to new experiences while continually expanding on what they have discovered as mentors.

Accepting Mentorship as a Compass of Success

Technology has unleashed unimagined possibilities for connection and learning, making it simpler than ever to locate mentors worldwide. Virtual mentorship programs, online communities, and digital resources have revolutionized how mentors are approached, opening up endless doors of potential growth for both the mentor and mentee.

So, while we embrace new tools and technologies for mentorship, it's still vitally important to remember its core essence—relationships, connection, a shared journey of growth and empowerment. Trust, respect, and mutual learning still hold true whether mentoring someone offline or online.

Digital mentorship can be just as impactful in my work. Throughout my mentoring experiences with women and young people from diverse cultures spanning multiple countries through video calls, emails, and online platforms, my engagement has expanded my perspective while deepening my appreciation of global challenges and opportunities.

As time progresses, I remain committed to exploring innovative methods of mentoring and being mentored in today's digital environment. By harnessing technology as we do so, mentorship can reach further—creating a more connected and empowered society in its wake.

Steps for Becoming an Effective Mentor

Are you starting your mentorship journey? Below, I offer some practical steps I took to become an effective mentor. These may change with time as you gain experience, but nonetheless, they provide a solid framework upon which meaningful mentoring relationships may form.

1. **Active Listening:** One essential skill any mentor must master is active listening. Active listening goes beyond simply hearing what your mentee says—it involves understanding their needs, concerns, and aspirations without passing judgment. It gives each member of your mentee's community the space and respect they deserve to voice their opinions freely and independently. Take the time to actively

listen without judgment so your mentee knows their voice has been heard!

2. **Ask Thought-Provoking Questions:** A mentor's primary job is not to supply all the answers for their mentee but instead help them discover them themselves. Asking thoughtful questions that encourage introspection and critical thought processes among your mentees helps your mentor delve more deeply into their thoughts and emotions while stimulating critical thought for future decisions made by their mentees.

3. **Share Your Experiences:** Be bold and open up about your journey's successes and failures with your mentee; being vulnerable with them can build trust and rapport between both of you.

4. **Provide Constructive Feedback:** Feedback is critical for growth but must be delivered properly in order to be most beneficial. Focus on providing constructive comments that highlight improvement areas while acknowledging and celebrating strengths within their mentee's person.

5. **Encourage Self-Reflection:** Encourage your mentee to use reflection as an effective method for personal growth and increasing self-awareness. When used properly, reflection can provide immense potential benefits and deepen self-knowledge.

6. **Celebrate Their Achievements:** Acknowledging and celebrating your mentee's victories is crucial in building their confidence and reinforcing positive behaviors. Acknowledging achievements helps reinforce positive behaviors while building self-confidence.

7. **Be Patient & Supportive:** Growth takes time, so when setbacks arise, mentors and mentees should remain supportive and remind themselves that setbacks are an inevitable part of the learning process.

8. **Foster Independence:** Mentorship should provide your mentees with the confidence and tools they need to become independent, self-

sufficient individuals. Please encourage them to make decisions based on themselves alone while having faith in themselves and trusting in themselves and their capabilities.

Mentorship creates an ever-widening circle. When you mentor someone, you not only directly impact their life, but your influence also grows throughout their circle of influence. This effect creates lasting change while building communities of empowered individuals working toward a positive impact in our world.

One of the greatest joys of mentoring lies in seeing your mentees carry forward the lessons and values you've imparted. You see them mentor others with passion and dedication similar to what was shown to them. You know that your impactful mentorship will last beyond you, leaving an everlasting legacy of empowerment spanning generations.

As part of my work with Corazon and my personal life, I have witnessed firsthand the ripple effect mentorship has on the lives around me. One act can spark another and transform multiple lives through mentoring alone —this is truly amazing and represents its true power: making an impactful impression across communities that you may never fully comprehend!

Mentorship is one of the greatest gifts anyone can give; all it requires to be effective as a mentor is listening, sharing knowledge, and assisting on others' journey.

Mentorship can be an incredible catalyst for change—for mentors and mentees alike. Please take full advantage of its potential, share your light, and continue the journey, knowing its legacy will linger long into the future.

JULIE DELGADILLO

About Julie Delgadillo: Julie Delgadillo is a confident, enthusiastic, witty, and sought-after passionate servant leader and mentor with over 20 years of experience in non-profit management, leadership development, and confidence coaching. Julie is the Executive Director of Corazón U.S. & Mexico. Julie is a firm believer in leading by example and actively engages in developing community leaders. It's not uncommon to catch her rolling up her sleeves and wearing a toolbelt to personally contribute to building homes in Mexico for deserving low-income families.

Julie's strengths and passions are rooted in empowering women to be confidence in every area of their lives. Julie has personally coached and developed teens and women from across the globe and serves as an International Ambassador for the economic development of women. Julie is also a former International Beauty Queen and a long-time Hunger Relief Advocate.

An alumna of the prestigious University of Notre Dame's Mendoza School of Business Non-Profit Business Management Executive Leadership Program, Julie's educational journey is a testament to her commitment to growth and learning. Her undergraduate studies at Mount Saint Mary College and her certification in transformational life coaching from the Life Purpose Institute further enrich her holistic approach to empowerment. When she is not out conquering the world, you can find her discovering new brunch spots, listening to audiobooks, or in the aisles of T.J. Maxx, Marshall's, or HomeGoods. Let's Connect: *www.Linkedin.com/in/JulieDelgadillo*

Author's Website: *www.linktr.ee/SheConquersTheWorld*

Book Series Website: *www.TheBookOfMentors.com*

"WORK HARDER ON YOURSELF THAN YOU DO ON YOUR JOB."

~ JIM ROHN

KELLI HUDSON-KEY

LEANING INTO MENTORSHIP & LEGACY

Reflecting on my life, leadership, and professionalism, I realize that mentorship has been more than just a tool for personal and professional growth; it has been my guiding compass. Over the years, I have had the privilege of learning from some of the greatest minds in leadership, standing on the shoulders of giants, and passing on the invaluable lessons I've learned.

Jim Rohn once said, "Success is nothing more than a few simple disciplines, practiced every day." This quote has become the cornerstone of my approach to mentorship, life, and leadership. It reminds me that small, consistent actions are what pave the path to greatness.

The Heart of Mentorship: Matching Values

One of the most important lessons I've learned about mentorship is the necessity of aligning values. Finding the right mentor isn't solely about their accolades or achievements; ensuring that their values align with yours is essential. In my experience, I've approached mentorship like an interview process. I ask questions, observe actions, and make sure our values are compatible. This principle has shaped my selection of mentors and guided me in becoming a mentor to others.

I remember a time when I was looking for a new mentor. I admired their success, but something felt off. After an open conversation, I realized that their approach to work-life balance didn't align with my priorities. This was a crucial moment that highlighted the significance of values in mentorship. As mentors, we are responsible for setting an example, which starts with being authentic.

The Criticism Sandwich: Delivering Growth with Grace

One mentorship principle that I value highly is the "Criticism Sandwich." This method, exemplified in Jim Rohn's teachings, balances constructive feedback with encouragement. It involves starting with a compliment, then delivering the necessary correction, and finally closing with a positive note. This approach ensures that mentees feel supported while also being challenged to grow.

I recall mentoring a young woman early in her career. She was bright, ambitious, and full of potential but struggled with time management. During one of our conversations, I began by praising her creativity and drive. I then gently pointed out that her missed deadlines were affecting her progress. I concluded by expressing my confidence in her ability to overcome this challenge. Not only did she rise to the occasion, but she also began mentoring others on time management. That's the power of delivering growth with grace.

Generational Mentorship: Building a Legacy

Mentorship extends beyond the present moment; it creates a ripple effect that can influence future generations. Jim Rohn once said, "We are the average of the five people we spend the most time with." This concept has influenced my perspective on mentorship, prompting me to surround myself with inspiring individuals while also striving to be a source of inspiration for others.

One of my proudest moments was when my daughter decided to leave a secure job in film production to start her own company with her husband. Watching her embrace the unknown reminded me of the mentors who guided me through my leaps of faith. The lessons I've shared with her— such as the importance of setting goals and serving others—are now being passed down to her team and beyond. This experience serves as a reminder that mentorship is a legacy we build, one relationship at a time.

Leaning In: The Power of Adaptability

One principle I have embraced, particularly in recent years, is "leaning in." The world has undergone tremendous changes, and mentorship has also had to adapt. When COVID-19 struck, everything I understood about conducting business was turned upside down. I had to shift from in-person meetings to an entirely virtual format almost overnight.

Initially, the challenge felt overwhelming. However, as Jim Rohn often said, "Don't wish it were easier; wish you were better." I embraced the discomfort and learned to conduct Zoom meetings, train teams virtually, and maintain personal connections through a screen. By Easter that year, I had mastered Zoom and was teaching others to use it—ranging from my team and customers to my family. This experience taught me valuable lessons in adaptability, which I now share with every mentee I work with.

Mentorship Beyond the Professional

Over the years, I have learned to distinguish between helping and supporting. As mentors, our role isn't to do the work for our mentees; instead, we guide them as they navigate their paths. This approach empowers them to take ownership of their journeys, fostering independence and resilience.

I have witnessed this principle many times, but one moment stands out. A mentee of mine was struggling with self-doubt and was convinced she couldn't achieve her goals. Rather than offering her solutions, I chose to ask questions that guided her toward discovering her own answers.

Seeing her light up with newfound confidence reminded me of the power of support over simply providing help. As Zig Ziglar said, "A lot of people have gone further than they thought they could because someone else thought they could."

Confidence, Action, & Accountability

Throughout my career, I have identified three essential pillars for success: confidence, action, and accountability. These principles have been central to my mentorship philosophy and are often where I see the most resistance.

Confidence is the foundation of success. Without it, even the best-laid plans can fail.

The next step is **taking action**—leaping into the unknown, even when fear is present.

Accountability ensures consistency, holding us to our commitments to ourselves and others.

I frequently share these principles with my mentees, encouraging them to develop schedules, set measurable goals, and take daily actions toward achieving their dreams. One of my favorite quotes from Tom Landry encapsulates this idea: "The secret to winning is constant, consistent management." Success isn't derived from grand gestures but from showing up daily and putting in the effort.

Mentorship in a Post-Pandemic World

The world may appear different today, but the need for mentorship has grown even stronger. Many people feel more isolated, hesitant, and guarded. As mentors, we must adapt by finding new ways to connect and inspire them. This involves deepening our empathy, honing our communication skills, and embracing technology as a bridge rather than a barrier.

One of the most valuable lessons I've learned is that mentorship is not about achieving perfection; it's about making progress. It involves meeting people where they are and guiding them toward their aspirations. As John C. Maxwell says, "Leadership is influence—nothing more, nothing less." At its core, mentorship is the purest form of leadership.

The Future of Mentorship

As I contemplate the future, I feel a sense of hope. The principles championed by Jim Rohn—discipline, adaptability, and a commitment to adding value to others—are more relevant now than ever. By embracing these principles and continuing to evolve, we can ensure that mentorship remains a powerful catalyst for growth and change.

To everyone reading this, my message is straightforward: Don't wait. Don't wait to find a mentor, to become a mentor, or to take the next step in your journey. Life is short, and the impact you can have is immeasurable. Embrace the moment, take action, and never underestimate the power of mentorship to transform lives—beginning with your own.

KELLI HUDSON-KEY

About Kelli Hudson-Key: Kelli Hudson-Key has built a remarkable career that speaks volumes of her dedication, leadership, and passion. Currently, she holds the esteemed position of Senior Division Executive at Park Lane Jewelry. In this role, she plays an instrumental part in the company's growth and success, leading her team with a unique blend of wisdom and enthusiasm.

Before her tenure at Park Lane Jewelry, Kelli showcased her prowess in the realm of direct sales with Mary Kay Inc., a global powerhouse known for its impressive legacy spanning sixty years in the beauty industry. For over twenty two years, she contributed significantly to the brand as Senior Sales Director. During this time, Kelli was integral in fostering the company's sales strategies, solidifying its position as one of the leading direct sellers of personal beauty products in the United States.

Her longevity and success in the industry is a testament to Kelli's unparalleled drive and commitment. Her knack for understanding market dynamics, combined with her talent for nurturing and guiding her teams, has marked her as a leading figure in the direct sales sector. In every endeavor, Kelli Hudson-Key's name is synonymous with excellence, leadership, and an unwavering commitment to success around the world.

Message me at: *m.me/Kelli.HudsonKey*

Author's Website: *www.MyParkLane.com/KelliKey*

Book Series Website: *www.TheBookOfMentors.com*

"YOUR LEVEL OF SUCCESS WILL RARELY EXCEED YOUR LEVEL OF PERSONAL DEVELOPMENT."

~ JIM ROHN

LAUREN COBB

CHOOSING CHANGE, NOT CHANCE

When I was eighteen years old, I watched my father face the fight of his life against cancer. Those years shaped me in ways I never could have imagined. My dad was a man of quiet strength, someone who could light up a room with his laugh and smile.

When the diagnosis came, it was as though the universe had tipped sideways, but he refused to let his spirit follow. He became my first real example of how life doesn't get better by chance; it gets better by change.

Early in his treatment, one of Dad's closest friends and mentors sat with him in our living room—he himself was in a five-plus-year battle with cancer. He challenged my Dad to not only ride the roller coaster but find a way to enjoy it.

My Dad took that to heart. There was pain, yes, but also a spark of determination of "I'll enjoy the ride."

From that day on, his perspective changed. It didn't mean the battle got any easier. The pain was real, the treatments grueling, and the outcome inevitable. But he decided that if his time was limited, he'd spend it being a light to others. Dad surrounded himself with positivity, and he shared it with everyone around him—from the nurses administering his radiation to the single adults in his congregation that he chose to still lead during his battle.

The Power of Perspective

One of the most profound lessons I learned from my dad was that change starts within. He couldn't change his diagnosis or his prognosis, but he could change how he faced it. That shift in mindset was transformative, not just for him but for everyone around him. He became a beacon of hope and resilience, even on the hardest days.

Those times together became much more cherished. I was always a Daddy's girl. As a young girl, I was up early in the mornings on weekends to go grab breakfast at the grocery store and go turn the irrigation gates and follow it down the ditches for miles until it reached the lane where my uncles and brothers were waiting to get it into the yards and orchard.

The way we discovered his cancer was due to an injury he got while on a camping trip with me and my then-boyfriend. We took a week and drove through the beautiful back country roads of Canyonlands National Park in Utah. We would drive all day, off-roading and stopping to see the beautiful views, and then stop to set up camp before dark and cook dinner. The three of us were traveling with my Dad's boss, his wife, and his son, who came from Alabama to explore Southern Utah.

One morning, we were getting camp set up, and Dad reached into the back of the truck bed to lift out a bin of gear, and a sudden pop and shooting pain in the back of his shoulder quickly radiated through his whole arm. It was *so* painful for him. We got his arm as stable as we could and went about our day. Thankfully, it happened toward the end of the trip.

We ended up skipping the last night of camping and driving eight hours home that night. After a few weeks of doctor appointments, it was confirmed that he had kidney cancer, a cancer that initiates from the kidney and then attacks the bones. That pop we had heard was actually a tumor that popped and tore his rotator cuff at the same time. That led to the life-changing events I mentioned above.

Those times together are cherished, and the lessons he taught me throughout my life have stuck with me. He wasn't just a say-er; he was the do-er as well. On that particular trip, we would switch off drivers between the three of us: Dad, Ty (my boyfriend and now husband), and myself.

I was behind the wheel of his brand-new King Ranch F-150, driving through these canyon roads. It isn't the canyon as you might picture; Southern Utah is desert—BEAUTIFUL desert. This canyon road was narrow, with a rock wall on the right side of the truck and a cliff to the left of the truck—so narrow that looking out my driver's window, I could not see the road.

Our tire was on the very edge of the red dirt road. I FROZE. I immediately put the truck in park, climbed out of the driver's seat, and into the back seat next to Ty. My dad was in the front passenger seat. It was silence for a second, and then my Dad said, "Lauren, get back up here."

I gave my excuse, and he replied calmly and kindly, "You have to learn how to do this. I will talk you through it, but you have to get back up here because neither Ty nor I can climb over these seats into the driver's seat." Mind you, we could not open any of the vehicle doors because we were so close to the rock wall, and the other side was on the cliff.

I gathered my emotions and climbed back into the driver's seat. Not totally calm, but I was there, and my Dad talked me through it. We made it up the hill and to the overlook safely. Talk about life lessons.

Choosing to Be a Light

It wasn't always easy for Dad to be positive. There were days when the pain was overwhelming and his body felt like a prison. But even on those days, he made a conscious effort to focus on gratitude.

"Gratitude is the antidote to despair." He kept a journal where he wrote three things he was grateful for and experiences he had. Some days, the entries were simple. Other days, they were more profound.

This practice didn't erase his pain, but it shifted his focus. It reminded him that even in the darkest moments, there was still light to be found. And that light was contagious. People who came to visit often left feeling uplifted, even when they had come to comfort him. He had a way of turning the focus outward, asking about their lives, celebrating their joys, and consoling their sorrows. He chose to be a light, even as his own life dimmed.

Carrying the Torch

When Dad passed away, the grief was immense. But amidst the tears, there was also a profound sense of gratitude. He had shown me that life is not about the number of days we have but about how we live them. His legacy became a compass for my own life.

As I grew older, I found myself drawing on the lessons he taught me on a daily. When I battled postpartum depression, I remembered Dad's words about gratitude.

In my career as an entrepreneur, there have been countless challenges. Starting a business is like navigating a storm with no map, but I've learned to embrace the ride. I've surrounded myself with positivity, just as Dad did, and sought out mentors who challenge me to grow. I've made it a point to uplift others and to be a light in my community because I know firsthand how transformative that can be.

Life by Change

Jim Rohn's words, "Your life does not get better by chance, it gets better by change," resonate deeply with me. My dad's journey taught me that change is not always about grand gestures. Sometimes, it's about small, deliberate choices: to be grateful, to be kind, to focus on what you can control rather than what you can't.

Change is hard. It requires courage and resilience. But it's also where growth happens. My dad could have chosen to let his illness define him, to give in to bitterness and despair. Instead, he chose to redefine his life on his own terms, to find joy in the midst of pain, and to leave a legacy of love and light.

Today, when challenges arise, I remind myself that I have the power to choose—to change my perspective, to seek out the light, and to be a light for others. Life may not always be fair, but it is always precious. And the way we live it is up to us.

So, here's to change. To gratitude. To choose joy, even on the hardest days. And to live a life that's better—not by chance, but by the deliberate, beautiful act of change.

LAUREN COBB

About Lauren Cobb: Lauren Cobb is a wife to her amazing and supportive husband Tyler, and a mother to three beautiful daughters who've taught her more in the last twelve years than she has learned in the first twenty-three years of her life.

At a young age, Lauren knew she had a lot of ambition and drive. As she became an adult, she knew that entrepreneurship was her passion, and thankfully, she married someone who supported that! Together with Ty, they own a graphic and media design company that they've built from the ground up. Growing and seeing the successes of their own efforts has been one of the most rewarding experiences!

Self-development and leadership have been a big part of Lauren's life since she was fourteen. She traveled and taught leadership to youth across the country throughout her high school years. She knows first-hand how self-development is crucial to success in life. Knowing who you are and finding your purpose and passion is important.

As Lauren and her husband Ty are building their businesses and seeking a network and friends who are aligned with their values, they've found in Champion Circle and learned how to properly mastermind. Lauren is a member of the corporate executive team at Champion Circle Networking Association, founded and led by Jon Kovach Jr. Masterminds have changed her life and her business for the better.

Author's Website: *www.TyCobb.MyPortfolio.com*

Book Series Website: *www.TheBookOfMentors.com*

"GIVING IS BETTER THAN RECEIVING BECAUSE GIVING STARTS THE RECEIVING PROCESS."

~ JIM ROHN

LIZ SEARS

THE ART OF INSPIRING OTHERS

Actions speak louder than words, and energy speaks louder than action. Maya Angelou famously said, "I've learned that people will forget what you said, people will forget what you did, but people will never forget how you made them feel."

There is an art to making people "feel" inspired. This art is also a skill set that can be learned, practiced, and honed to be a powerful influence for good. And this art has two parts: gratitude and example.

One Sunday, when I was in church, we had a lesson about gratitude. As Christians, we're taught in the Bible to "give thanks in all circumstances." So, to generate a good discussion on the subject, the teacher asked, "What is the opposite of gratitude?" No one answered for a moment, and we all sat there thinking. It was an excellent question.

As we pondered the question, I suddenly had an epiphany and raised my hand. When she called on me, I said, "Judgement is the opposite of gratitude."

She looked at me with a startled look, clearly having not considered that perspective before, and asked me to share what I meant. I said, "When we judge something as being wrong in some way or not what it's supposed to be, we cannot feel gratitude. If we think something shouldn't have happened the way it did or that someone shouldn't have said or reacted how they did, we don't feel gratitude; instead, we feel judgment in our hearts."

The discussion continued with the class, and I sat there thinking more about that epiphany. I decided to pay attention to that over the next week or so. In each situation and conversation, I considered if I was feeling gratitude or judgment, and it was startling how often I felt judgment in my heart about the smallest things. It was so subtle that I didn't notice until I purposely paid attention.

Reframing the perspective from judgment to gratitude was much more difficult than I had imagined! If I wanted to follow the command to "give thanks in all circumstances," I would need to figure this out.

I remember walking into my kitchen the next morning, seeing the dishes and mess left on the table, and thinking, "Sheesh! How hard is it to put your dish in the dishwasher and wipe up the crumbs? Ugh, I wish my son would just clean up after himself without me constantly reminding him."

My next thought was, "Oh! Yeah. I just experienced judgment." But at that moment, I couldn't figure out how to give thanks without violating my desire to have a clean home. Should I just ignore that he made a mess and walked away? What kind of mom would I be if I didn't teach my son to clean up after himself? This shift from judgment to gratitude was not easy!

After thinking about it for a while, I realized I could feel gratitude while also taking action for a different outcome. I chose to feel gratitude that there was food for my son to eat, gratitude that he was capable of getting his own breakfast, gratitude for this opportunity to teach him, and so on.

Then I called him back into the kitchen and with an attitude of gratitude and without judgment I said, "Hey bud, don't forget to clean up after yourself when you're done in the kitchen. And when you do, that's really nice of you because then everyone else in the house gets to enjoy a clean home too. Thanks so much! Love you!"

Okay, that felt different! I was so used to feeling in my heart that he was wrong, that it was so strange and foreign to have this conversation where I didn't feel judgment. It was so strange to have this conversation while feeling gratitude. It felt lighter. I felt a connection to my son at that moment that wasn't ever there before when I talked to him about leaving a mess that the rest of us had to deal with.

Then, later that day, I was hurrying to get something done and drove to the store to grab something really quick. And I hit every red light! I started to feel frustrated and then thought, "Oh! Yeah. I just experienced judgment...again." And again, I couldn't figure out how to give thanks when I was about to be late for my next commitment.

So, I took a breath and thought, "I'm so grateful to be in a car and to be able to drive to the store." Then I decided to express pre-gratitude for a parking spot right up front, and you won't believe it! But I pulled in and there literally was a parking spot right up front. I didn't have any feeling of expectation; I only had a feeling of gratitude. And I could feel the connection.

One of the strongest memories I have of choosing gratitude over judgment was on a Saturday night. I had just bought a new rug to go under my dining room table. I know it's dumb to have a rug under a table where people are eating because it's destined to have food spilled on it, but it looks so good!

Anyway, my sister was over visiting, and while we were talking, I dished up a plate of food at the island, turned around to take it to the table, and somehow I clipped the edge of the table with the edge of my plate, and this completely full plate of food toppled right onto my new rug. I sighed, shrugged, and bent down to pick up as much of the food as I could. Then I asked her to give me a second while I grabbed my little Bissell. We continued our conversation while I spot-cleaned the rug.

She told me later that my example had an impact on her that day. Like any normal person, she was in the habit of getting angry or frustrated when things like that happened, yet because I'd been practicing choosing gratitude, I had unknowingly set an example that inspired her.

Over the years, the more I work on gratitude instead of judgment, the more surprised I am at how it affects my interactions with others. There's more peace, more connection, more graciousness we all feel. It's really something!

Part one of this art of inspiring others is gratitude; part two is being an example.

Being an example doesn't mean being perfect. Being an example means that as you work to create a life you love, others see that and want to do the same.

I've found that the most rewarding part of life is when I get to witness how something I have done made someone else's life better. I've also found that this happens most often when I approach life with this perspective:

My responsibility is to create more than I need so that I can use my excess to bless others.

Could you imagine what the world would look like if every person on earth embraced this perspective?

Nearly twenty-two years after moving out of my first home, I received a thank-you card in the mail from a woman who, as a teenager, lived in that neighborhood where I had the privilege of teaching her class at our local church. The card she wrote read, "Dear Liz, I wanted to thank you for being a positive influence in my youth. I don't ever remember specific interactions, but I know you were someone who cared about me and showed interest in my life. When I look back, you are one of the only leaders I remember. Thank you for your example and involvement in my life."

It is so true what Maya Angelou said, "I've learned that people will forget what you said, people will forget what you did, but people will never forget how you made them feel."

You never know who might be watching you. You never know the impact you may have on someone. And you have a much farther reach than you know. Each interaction is an opportunity to be an inspiration to others.

Each moment is an opportunity to choose how you experience your life. I wish you a life of abundance where you consistently witness how the world and others are better because of you.

LIZ SEARS

About Liz Sears: Liz Sears lives her life in every way to fulfill her life mission, which is to "inspire the masses to live lives full of connection, contribution, adventure, and impact." As a speaker and writer, she focuses on the consistency of striving toward becoming the best version of ourselves and sharing how to be awake and engaged in life. She fully believes that life, with its extensive variety of obstacles and opportunities, can be an amazing adventure. It's all about how we play the hand we were dealt and what we choose to create.

Liz has been married to her best friend since 1996, and together, they have raised four wonderful sons. She is a proud alumna of Kent-Meridian High School and pursued Business Administration/Management at the University of Utah. Her roots trace back to Seattle, Washington, but she and her family now call Layton, Utah home.

Beginning in the financial industry in 1995, Liz's career path has included roles such as Mortgage Loan officer, Property Manager, Real Estate Investor, and most recently as Team Leader and Associate Broker of Utah's Elite | REALTORS® at Real Brokers, LLC. She has served many times in leadership roles in the Real Estate industry, including on the Board of Directors for the Northern Wasatch Association of Realtors and as a Governing Board Member of the Women's Council of Realtors Utah.

Author's Website: *www.UtahsEliteRealtors.com*

Book Series Website: *www.TheBookOfMentors.com*

"IF YOU DON'T DESIGN YOUR OWN LIFE PLAN, CHANCES ARE YOU'LL FALL INTO SOMEONE ELSE'S PLAN. AND GUESS WHAT THEY HAVE PLANNED FOR YOU? NOT MUCH."

~ JIM ROHN

M. A. FULTS

THE ESSENTIAL CONNECTOR

"It is the set of the sails, not the direction of the wind, that determines which way we will go."
~ Jim Rohn

I confess that this particular Jim Rohn quote was chosen based more on my love of the sea than on the topic of this chapter.

"For things to change, YOU have to change.
For things to get better, YOU have to get better.
For things to improve, YOU have to improve.
When YOU grow, EVERYTHING in your life grows with you."
~ Jim Rohn

In this final Book of Mentors, honoring the great Jim Rohn, I want to circle back to something that has been included in every previous chapter: the importance of relationships. If Legacy Stones are stones placed by others or ourselves along the paths we walk in life, then relationships are the connecting earth, often holding the Stones in place.

Whether the Stones are there from memories of mentors or friends, family or acquaintances, teachers or students, or whether they are from books or videos, actors or writers, the best-laid Stones, the Stones with the most import, are connected—and they stay connected through relationships.

We choose each path, each Stone, upon which we walk. We also choose how often we revisit a Stone, abandon a Stone, or whether we turn completely around to take a different path with different Stones. Most often, I've chosen a path based on who and what is happening in my present life, albeit formed by past experiences and even past relationships. But what about those times when my path 'choice' seemingly has not been my own? When others, circumstances, or life's inevitable ups and downs have seemed to force my course or my change of course?

In those times, I always remember the Viktor Frankl quote heard long ago.

Viktor Frankl, concentration camp survivor and father of Anne Frankl (Frank), said in his book, *Man's Search for Meaning,* "Everything can be taken from a man but one thing: the last of the human freedoms—to choose one's attitude in any given set of circumstances, to choose one's own way." Essentially, to choose the path to take in response to that person, that circumstance, that up or down. Or, to paraphrase Danny Silk, to choose to "control my freakin' self."

Frankl was right that we can and do "choose [our] own way" by controlling only ourselves, not attempting to control or manipulate others, and choosing our own path. For me, choosing my own path and exerting control over only myself, not others, has led to the best relationships, the happiest of relationships—to lifetime relationships.

At the end of our lives, experiences, memories, and relationships matter. Relationships are all that matter, whether or not we acknowledge that fact. Some might argue that relationships are secondary, not as important as reputation, social status, or the acquisition of 'stuff,' but if the Stones we place on the paths we trod mean anything—if the mentors we choose to follow and allow to influence our lives matter—then relationships are the cement that holds those Stones in place.

Fifty-five years ago, I made a choice that has been the foundation of every relationship, every path, and every Stone upon those paths. I chose to surrender in order to find freedom. I chose to surrender to a Master and a Savior; to a Godhead, Three in One.

Within that one relationship alone, I find that I can control myself with ease, peace, joy, and love as a direct result of that decision. And the wonder of it all, when I don't try to control others, or even Him—and yes, I have tried to manipulate Jesus—He just smiled and, firmly and gently, brought me back to the center, wherein lies the Love, the Joy, and the Peace. When I control myself, I find relationships with friends who, in time, become family.

> *"Let others lead small lives, but not you.*
> *Let others argue over small things, but not you.*
> *Let others cry over small hurts, but not you.*
> *Let others leave their future in someone else's hands, but not you."*
> ~ Jim Rohn

In the last two and a half years, through stepping onto some new Stones, a new path has been chosen and walked—a new path wherein I have grown and changed exponentially for the better. Specifically, two new relationships, Stones if you will, two mentors, came into my life and are now firmly embedded in the path I walk.

The first mentor opened my eyes and heart to the Kingdom of God. Pedro Adao is an entrepreneur, marketer, coach, leader, and movement-maker extraordinaire. He spent many years listening to and learning from Myles Munroe about the Kingdom of God and still listens to Munroe tapes for hours on end. Pedro passes along the Kingdom of God teachings through his multiple programs, helping people find and fulfill their dreams and aspirations.

One of the programs I joined with him required reading Myles Munroe's book, *Rediscovering the Kingdom*. When I finally did, my mind was blown, my heart expanded, and I began to walk in the Kingdom. Last year, Pedro conducted a workshop on becoming a Movement Maker; my takeaway from that workshop was that "I Am A Kingdom Walker."

Erik Swanson is another mentor who has impacted my life, my chosen path, as much as Pedro has. I joined a couple of Erik's Masterminds over a year ago. In that time, he has introduced me to mentors (as I've stated in other books, most of them I'd never even heard of) and authors, speakers, and entrepreneurs. These were people in fields and walks of life that I had never known or encountered personally, and now I've spoken with them, laughed with them, and even cried with them. Recently, though, he asked a question during a Mastermind: essentially, he asked us to take a few minutes and develop a motto or theme for our lives.

It didn't take me long. I knew that Love would be part of it, because Love is a huge part of who I am and who I desire to be from the inside out. And my first thought was, "Love Conquers All." Only that didn't fit —it was kind of 'old,' overused, and didn't fully meet what was in my heart to say.

Very quickly, I heard—sensed? Realized?—that what I was searching for, what fully encompassed the theme for my life, was "Love Provides." Thank you, Erik, for helping me formulate something I didn't even know I wanted to.

To bring this full circle: Two Stones, same path, connected through relationships—precious, intimate relationships with multiple people I now call friends, many of whom I also call family. In the end, it is our relationships and our time with others we love and care about that matters the most.

The relationships that continue through life are with my brother, who left this earth forty-four years ago, my mother thirty-one years ago, my father nineteen years ago, and my sister three years ago—they are and will forever be my brother, mother, father, sister. Memories of our times together live on in my heart, and now, thanks to Erik, in books.

I can't tell you of the toys I've possessed—I don't remember them; they sit in closets—or the honors I've received and the words spoken over or about me, or even that I've spoken to others, as they have, for the most part, fallen away. But the people and the relationships have lasted; they are remembered and they matter.

"Love Provides" struck a chord with many of those in attendance at the Mastermind, even Erik Swanson. I don't know what specifically it meant to them, but for me, that chord was one of abundance and growth, needs and desires, giving and receiving.

Holy Scriptures tell us:

God is Love
Perfect Love Casts Out All Fear
God is Perfect Love

"Love Provides"

M. A. FULTS

About M. A. (MaryAlice) Fults: Born into an Army family, and with thirty nine years serving in and then working for the US Navy, Fults spent many years traveling and living in foreign countries including four years in Teheran, Iran. She has a BFA in Drama Production from the University of AZ and a MS in Management from Naval Postgraduate School in Monterey, CA.

After retiring for the second time in 2022, Fults continued her life-long pursuit of learning, embarking on her new found passion of Heart Healing, Financial Advising and Life-Coaching. She has been blessed with one son.

Book Series Website: *www.TheBookOfMentors.com*

"SET THE KIND OF GOALS THAT WILL MAKE SOMETHING OF YOU TO ACHIEVE THEM."

~ JIM ROHN

MARIS SEGAL & KEN ASHBY

THE TRUE EVIDENCE OF LIFE IS GROWTH

It is impossible to write about personal development without honoring Jim Rohn! He was such an influential American entrepreneur, author, and motivational speaker who has inspired millions worldwide. As a couple in love and in business together for over twenty years, we are certainly the beneficiaries of Jim Rohn's teaching and mentorship. Rohn's work has helped guide our personal leadership journey and our Relational and Conscious Leadership work with businesses large and small.

First, Jim Rohn's teachings emphasize key life actions and ways of being that we are all striving to master. These include goal setting, accountability, discipline, consistency, and surrounding oneself with positive influences. Second, one of his most significant perspectives is the importance of personal growth and continuous learning. Whether personally or professionally, Jim Rohn noted that "investing in self-education, self-reflection, and skill development is the gateway to unleashing a person's capabilities."

> *"Work harder on yourself than you do on your job."*
> ~ Jim Rohn

This quote resonates deeply with us. We coach our clients to always be in the mindset that "the only true evidence of life is growth." Growth happens from the inside out, and that's what makes great heart-centered and purpose-driven leaders. Being curious and in discovery of yourself first opens doors to vision and accomplishments and enrolling the support of others.

We are in relationships with someone or something 24/7 at home, at work, and in our communities. If we are growing, our relationships with ourselves and others are always evolving for the better. If we are not in a continuous process of a growth mindset and expanding out of our comfort zone, we are likely to be comfortable and complacent. Not nurturing or challenging ourselves can stunt growth, leading to reduced productivity, depression, anxiety, and loneliness.

Imagine a garden or golf course left untended without water or care—eventually, it wilts and withers. This mirrors what happens to our families or teams if we neglect them. Choosing a growth mindset daily nurtures our relationships and shapes our future.

Have you encountered folks in your circle who have labeled themselves as "long in the tooth," "over the hill," or "glad to be on the top side of the grass?" Our perspective is that age is a number, not a destination! As we embrace the wisdom that comes with each daily experience and each passing year, we've made a solemn vow to never refer to ourselves as "old." Instead, we can simply say we're "experiencing extended adolescence" or "maturing like a fine wine."

Our commitment to life and each other is simple: as we continue maturing, we keep being curious, keep expanding our comfort zones, and lead with our hearts to keep touching lives. That's choosing a growth mindset and growth heart-set.

One Swing at a Time!

Ken: Let me tell you about my secret weapon in this game of life and, more specifically, my game of golf. While those nimble thirty-something-year-old golfers are busy mastering their swings, I've set my sights on a loftier goal: to shoot my age on the course. Shooting my age would mean playing 18-holes, scoring just four strokes over par—and that would be amazing! The best part is that it's a goal that keeps getting easier with each passing year! I mean, who needs a hole-in-one when you can celebrate a score that matches your birth year, right?

The beauty of Jim Rohn's philosophy is that it's like having a perpetual membership to the School of Growth. Every time I pick up a new skill for my golf game or experiment with a swing that may be out of my comfort zone, it's like pressing the reset button on my zest for life. Learning, evolving, and discovering new passions—this is what keeps me feeling energized and in committed action! No matter your age, growing with every experience is the ultimate adventure. So, choose to embrace the thrill of the journey and level up with each passing year.

Maris: Alright, I am going to continue Ken's golf metaphor for the game of life. I've always been athletic and love trying new things. Growing up, I was a sprinter, a figure skater, and a water ski pyramid climber; over the years, I shifted more towards hiking and snow skiing. A few years ago, with no prior experience other than many years of playing miniature golf as a kid and "putting" the ball through the clown's mouth, I chose golf as my new sport.

Ken and I have worked over the years with some of the nation's top celebrated golfers and golf courses, and I caught the bug and wanted to learn, especially to play with Ken! Now dedicated to chasing the little white (or pink) ball in the serenity of nature on an 18-hole golf course, I recently played in my first tournament, a fundraiser for our Kiwanis service club. Often my own worst enemy and very self-competitive, imagine me stepping onto the course, armed with determination and a healthy dose of Jim Rohn's personal growth philosophies.

Having only played a full 18-hole course once in my life, I was clear about my intention: "Play all eighteen holes without passing out from exhaustion, only lose three balls, and above all else, have fun." So, I'm at the driving range and preparing, and this is what it's like: You've got your set-up stance—like doing yoga with a club in hand. Then there's the swing—think of it as the perfect blend of elegance and controlled chaos, aiming for that elusive sweet spot: the center of the small golf ball. And don't even get me started on "putting"—it's like a delicate ballet of precision, perception, and nerve. All that said, I had an absolute blast and was in constant discovery!

Let's explore all the personal growth that happens on the course with lessons that apply to every aspect of life. With a positive mindset, every good shot and every missed shot is an opportunity to see and acknowledge what was working and what was not working. It's an opportunity to adjust for improvement without blaming the weather, the wind, or some distraction for causing the missed shot. And, by all means, it's a chance to avoid kicking myself—it leaves a mark.

Embracing the journey means celebrating small victories, like not accidentally hitting someone with my ball. Imagine how this applies to your life, personally and professionally. So, here's to all aspiring golfers, pickleballers, new hires, Chat GPT users, and anyone living in curiosity, going full speed into your world of personal growth and focusing on one swing at a time!

Swinging with Discipline & Consistency

In his book, *The Art of Exceptional Living*, Jim Rohn emphasizes a positive attitude and the power of "discipline and consistency." We prioritize "discipline and consistency" in everything we do, from leadership challenges with Fortune 100 clients to everyday tasks like writing, training prep, or organizing a closet at home. The key is not solely in achieving the end result; it's also in the satisfaction of knowing we set an intention, built a plan, and, with discipline, were consistently taking the necessary action steps to complete the intention in excellence.

This mindset also underscores the importance of intentionality and follow-through in all aspects of life. Again, relating to golf: one of our instructors, Laird Small, Director of Golf at Pebble Beach, says to approach every shot using this acronym, "NATO"—Not Attached to Outcome. Instead of focusing on the result, be attached to the intention, consistency, and discipline of our effort. Along the way, it is equally important to be present and acknowledge each step.

We are sure Jim Rohn would agree that being an all-in "player" in golf and in life is a pervasive mental game! Top PGA pro Rory McIlroy says, "Your mind is your ultimate golf club." Golf legend Arnold Palmer expressed it this way, "Success in golf depends less on strength of body than upon strength of mind and character." You can have all the latest equipment, and if you don't have a good mindset, you won't be able to execute your swings successfully.

So here we are, soaking up Jim Rohn's insights like a sponge and striving to embody his work and live in excellence. You can't go wrong with a golf bag full of great mindset clubs: a "goal setting" driver, a pitching wedge of "accountability," and a putter imbued with "discipline and consistency."

It all begins with vision and intention! The only true evidence of growth is your daily life! Live life fully, love life fully, and choose to grow. Here's to swinging for success, both on and off the green.

MARIS SEGAL & KEN ASHBY

About Maris Segal & Ken Ashby: Ken Ashby and Maris Segal, "America's Master Connectors," coach, consult, and collaborate with executives, entrepreneurs, celebrities and rising leaders to identify and bring their professional, personal, and philanthropic vision to life. Spanning four decades and forty countries, they combine their relationship marketing expertise with head and heart leadership to build meaningful connections and impactful strategies that drive their client's internal and external success.

Ken and Maris live by the philosophy, "We are all connected as humans first, and that's where the bottom line begins."

Together and individually, working across the public and private sectors, they have served a wide spectrum of local and global leaders, consumer and financial brands, causes, and policymakers. This dynamic duo also leverages Ken's international award-winning singer-songwriting gifts to develop collaborative teams with a songwriting workshop series. From board rooms and classrooms to Harvard, the White House, and Super Bowl Halftimes, Ken and Maris are also known for uniting diverse populations with innovative cross-cultural marketing and personal development programs.

As certified Executive and Relationship coaches, their latest book, *The RFactor; Universal Rhythms for Leading Prosperous Relationships* and their DRIVE method: Desire, Relationships, Intention, Vision, and Empowerment sit at the core of their work. Ashby and Segal set a path for every client to build high performing businesses and elevate personal and professional leadership for maximum impact and a 360-degree thriving life! As authors they have been featured in thirteen Amazon Bestselling leadership centered books. They speak regularly and were recently featured on the TEDx Farmingdale stage.

Author's Website: *www.SegalLeadershipGlobal.com*

Book Series Website: *www.TheBookOfMentors.com*

MEL CARR

BRICK BY BRICK: BUILDING SUCCESS WITH INTENTIONAL EFFORT

My business was built not on big, overnight wins but on consistent, intentional effort. At Cloversy, we don't chase quick fixes or viral moments. We offer our clients consistent, reliable support that helps them build strong foundations and long-term success. It's not always flashy, but it works—and it's how I've built my business and life.

I've always believed in the power of small actions done well. When I came across Jim Rohn's teachings, I was struck by how much his philosophies mirrored my own. While I don't claim to be a Jim Rohn expert, some of his most popular ideas—about consistency, relationships, and growth—feel like they're part of my DNA.

This chapter isn't about following Jim's path but about how his simple truths connect to how I operate Cloversy and how we serve our clients daily.

Small Steps, Big Impact

Jim Rohn once said, *"Success is nothing more than a few simple disciplines practiced every day."* That's how I run Cloversy. The way we show up for our clients isn't about significant changes or giant leaps. It's about the little things we do daily that build trust and deliver results.

For example, managing a client's inbox or calendar is not just about keeping things organized. It's about showing up consistently—replying on time, updating schedules, and anticipating their needs before they even ask. These tasks might seem small, but they add up. Over time, they create a level of trust that allows our clients to focus on what they do best while we handle the rest.

This belief in small, intentional steps has guided how I've grown Cloversy. When I first started, I didn't have it all figured out. I focused on doing one thing at a time well—building a process, hiring the right team member, or learning how to support a new client. It's like building a wall: you lay one brick, then another, and eventually, you have something solid and strong.

Who You Surround Yourself With Matters

One of Jim's most famous ideas is, *"You are the average of the five people you spend the most time with."* That idea resonates with me. I've always believed that the people around us shape who we are and how we grow.

At Cloversy, I've intentionally surrounded myself with the right people —from my team to clients. I don't just look for people with skills; I look for people who care, want to grow, and believe in doing good work.

Take Lindsey, my right-hand assistant for Six-Figure Chicks. Lindsey didn't just come in to check off tasks. She came in with energy, ideas, and a drive to help me grow this business. People like her don't just make Cloversy better—they make *me* better. And that's the kind of influence I want in my life.

The same goes for our clients. We work with entrepreneurs, leaders, and visionaries who inspire us to level up every day. Their passion pushes us to do our best work, and their trust allows us to be part of their success stories. That's why I'm so intentional about who we work with—it's about finding people who make us better.

Learning as You Go

Jim said, "Formal education will make you a living; self-education will make you a fortune." That feels so true to me. I didn't start Cloversy knowing everything about running a business. I've learned as I've gone along, picking up lessons from clients, mentors/coaches, and even mistakes.

When I started working on the Six-Figure Chicks book series, I had no idea how to publish a book. But I dove in, asked questions, delegated the right tasks, and figured it out one step at a time. Now, it's not just a book series—it's a movement helping women share their stories and grow their influence. That never would've happened if I wasn't willing to learn.

This mindset of constant learning is something I've built into Cloversy. I encourage my team to stay curious, try new things, and keep improving. Whether it's mastering a new tool, understanding a client's industry, or just finding a better way to get things done, learning is part of who we are.

Taking Care of Yourself

One of the most important lessons I've learned from Jim Rohn and my own experiences is that personal growth fuels professional success. Jim said, "Work harder on yourself than you do on your job." That's something I try to live by.

For me, this means starting each day with intention. I take a few moments in the morning to set goals, say my mission statements, and look at my vision board. These small habits ground me and help me show up as my best self—for my team, clients, and family.

It also means knowing when to step back. Running Cloversy is a lot of responsibility, but I've learned that rest is just as crucial as hustle.

Whether working out or hiking to clear my head, those moments recharge me and help me stay focused on what matters most.

Creating a Legacy

At the end of the day, what drives me is the idea of making a difference. Jim often talked about leaving a legacy, and that's something I think about a lot. For me, it's not just about building a successful business—it's about creating something that helps others grow and thrive.

That's why I started *Her Write to Rise,* a nonprofit that empowers women to heal and grow through writing. It's an extension of the Six-Figure Chicks series and a way to give back. Through Her Write to Rise, we're helping women share their stories, find their confidence, and see what's possible for their lives.

Legacy isn't about what you accomplish; it's about how you make others feel and what you leave behind. I hope to carry that in everything I do—at Cloversy, with Six-Figure Chicks, and in life.

The Golden Nugget

If there's one thing I want you to take away from this chapter, it's this: Success doesn't come from one big moment. It comes from small, consistent actions, meaningful relationships, and a willingness to grow. Whether running a business, writing a book, or chasing a dream, the key is to keep showing up.

At Cloversy, we've built everything brick by brick, with intentional effort and a focus on what really matters. You don't have to do it all at once. Just take the next step, then the one after that. Before you know it, you'll see how far you've come. That's the kind of success that lasts. And that's the kind of success I believe in.

MEL CARR

About Mel Carr: Mel Carr stands as a testament to the essence of profound introspection and self-awareness. She consistently dedicates time to understanding herself and those around her, seeking out beauty, meaning, and purpose in every facet of life. With an inherent ability to perceive what's "above and beyond" mere limitations, Mel's life resonates deeply with gratitude, humor, playfulness, and a graceful acceptance of the uncontrollable. Her innate curiosity allows her to unearth fresh and startling ideas, enabling her to engage wholeheartedly with life's mysteries and the sacred elements it holds.

As the esteemed Founder and Director of Cloversy, Mel possesses an uncanny understanding of time management and decision-making processes, irrespective of the content or environment. She's an emblem of organizational prowess, always at the forefront, ensuring every business need is met with precision and care. Mel's adeptness in resolving conflicts, enhancing brainstorming sessions, and fostering creativity sets her apart in the industry. She's ever attentive to customer feedback, ensuring prompt responses and resolutions to their queries. Infusing businesses with a fresh outlook and innovative ideas, Mel Carr is the catalyst that many organizations need to transcend their limitations. If you're looking to elevate your business, connecting with Mel is a promising pathway to boundless potential.

Author's Website: *www.Cloversy.com*

Book Series Website: *www.TheBookOfMentors.com*

DR. ONIKA SHIRLEY

RESILIENCE IN THE FACE OF ADVERSITY

"Discipline is the bridge between goals and accomplishment."
~ Jim Rohn

Life has a way of throwing unexpected challenges our way, and for me, those challenges came before I even graduated high school. I faced not one, but two car wrecks that shook the very foundation of my plans and aspirations. Each accident felt like a setback, a moment that could have easily led me to surrender to despair. Yet, deep down, a resilient spirit stirred within me. I recognized that these obstacles were not the end of my journey; rather, they were steppingstones that would ultimately lead me to greater heights.

The mindset I cultivated during those tumultuous times became my guiding light. I refused to let my circumstances define me. Instead, I embraced the philosophy that education and personal growth were my paths to empowerment. While others might have seen roadblocks, I viewed them as opportunities to learn, adapt, and rise above. It was this determination that propelled me back to school four years after my accidents.

As I embarked on my educational journey, I quickly learned the importance of discipline. The road ahead was not easy; it required immense effort, focus, and a commitment to my goals. But with each step I took—earning my associate's, bachelor's, and master's degrees—I felt a renewed sense of purpose and direction. I was not just acquiring knowledge; I was crafting a future built on resilience and hard work.

Through my experiences, I discovered that motivation can be sparked by the most challenging circumstances. It was a powerful reminder that we can choose how we respond to adversity. By honoring the lessons imparted by my own life, I aim to encourage readers to embrace their struggles as catalysts for growth.

In honoring the legacy of mentors like Jim Rohn, I encourage you to cultivate a mindset of resilience. Embrace discipline as a bridge to your dreams, and let your determination guide you through life's challenges. Remember, our journey is not defined by the setbacks we encounter but by how we rise from them.

As I moved forward in my education, I realized that learning extended far beyond the walls of a classroom. Each interaction, each setback, and each triumph contributed to my personal growth. They taught me that the seeds of success are sown in the soil of discipline and nurtured by a steadfast commitment to one's goals.

As I share my story, I hope it serves as a beacon of encouragement for you, the reader. Life's challenges are inevitable, but they do not have to define us. Instead, we can choose to rise, armed with the mindset that every setback is a setup for a comeback. Embrace education as a lifelong journey, cultivate discipline as a daily practice, and let motivation be the fuel that drives you toward your goals.

In honoring the teachings of mentors who have shaped my perspective, I invite you to reflect on your own journey. What challenges have you faced that tested your resolve? How have those experiences shaped your character and aspirations? Each of us has our own unique story, filled with trials and triumphs, and it is through these narratives that we find the strength to inspire ourselves and others.

Remember, it is not the circumstances that determine our futures, but our responses to those circumstances. Just as I learned to reframe my setbacks as opportunities for growth, you, too, can cultivate a mindset that embraces challenges as integral parts of your journey. The road to success is rarely a straight path; it winds and bends, often leading us through dark valleys before we reach the peaks of our potential.

Moreover, as you navigate your own path, don't underestimate the impact of giving back. As I progressed through my education and eventually entered the realm of academia, I realized the profound joy that comes from sharing knowledge and supporting others in their journeys. Mentorship became an essential part of my life. I found fulfillment in guiding students and peers, just as I had been guided by those who came before me. This cycle of learning and teaching is a powerful reminder that we are all interconnected, and our experiences can illuminate the paths of others.

As I reflect on my journey, I am reminded of Jim Rohn's wisdom: "Don't wish it were easier; wish you were better." This philosophy resonates deeply within me. It encourages us not to seek the absence of challenges but rather to strive for personal growth in the face of them. Each obstacle we encounter is an invitation to become better equipped for the future. Embrace this mindset, and you will find that you possess the tools to navigate any storm.

As you embark on this journey, remember that resilience is not just about enduring; it's about thriving. It is about embracing the lessons learned along the way, nurturing a mindset that welcomes growth, and contributing to the world around you. In this spirit, let's recap the key themes of this chapter and explore five actionable steps you can take to cultivate resilience and harness the power of education, discipline, and motivation in your own life.

Five Steps to Cultivate Resilience & Growth

1. **Embrace Lifelong Learning:** Commit to being a lifelong learner. Whether it's through formal education, online courses, or self-directed study, seek knowledge in areas that interest you. Set aside regular time each week to read, take courses, or engage with educational content that challenges your thinking and expands your

horizons. Remember that every bit of knowledge you acquire is a tool you can use to navigate life's challenges.

2. **Set Clear Goals:** Define what you want to achieve in your personal and professional life. Break these goals down into smaller, actionable steps. Write them down and revisit them regularly to track your progress. This practice not only provides clarity but also serves as a motivational tool, reminding you of what you are working toward, even during tough times.

3. **Develop a Positive Mindset:** Cultivating a positive mindset is essential for resilience. Begin each day with affirmations that reinforce your strengths and capabilities. When faced with setbacks, practice reframing negative thoughts into positive ones. Instead of saying, "I can't," shift to, "I can learn how." Surround yourself with positive influences—people, books, and media that uplift and inspire you.

4. **Build a Support Network:** Seek out mentors, peers, and friends who share your values and aspirations. Surround yourself with a supportive community that encourages your growth. Engage in conversations, share experiences, and learn from one another. This network will not only provide encouragement during challenging times but will also celebrate your successes with you.

5. **Practice Gratitude & Reflection:** Take time regularly to reflect on your experiences, both the challenges and the victories. Consider keeping a journal where you note what you are grateful for and the lessons learned from each experience. This practice helps you maintain perspective and recognize how far you have come, reinforcing your resilience and motivation.

As you integrate these steps into your life, remember that resilience is a journey, not a destination. It requires ongoing effort, reflection, and adaptation. By honoring your challenges and celebrating your growth, you will foster a mindset that empowers you to face whatever life throws your way.

As you embrace lifelong learning, set clear goals, develop a positive mindset, build a supportive network, and practice gratitude, you will not only cultivate resilience within yourself, but you will also inspire those around you. Your story—much like mine—has the power to uplift, encourage, and ignite the flame of determination in others.

In closing, remember that the world is full of possibilities, and your potential is boundless. Challenges will arise, but they are merely steppingstones on your journey toward fulfillment and success. As we honor the legacy of mentors like Jim Rohn, let us carry forward their teachings and embody the spirit of resilience.

Together, we can create a ripple effect of inspiration, fostering a community that uplifts and empowers one another. So, take your next step with confidence; the future awaits, and it is yours to shape.

DR. ONIKA SHIRLEY

About Dr. Onika L. Shirley: Dr. Onika L. Shirley is the Founder and CEO of Action Speaks Volume, Inc. She is a Procrastination Strategist and Behavior Change Expert and known for building unshakable confidence; stopping procrastination, and getting your dreams out of your head into your life. She is a Master Storyteller, International Speaker, Serves in Global Ministry, International Bestselling Author, International Award Recipient, Serial Entrepreneur, and Global Philanthropist impacting lives in the USA, Africa, India, and Pakistan.

Dr. O is a Motivational Speaker and Christian Counselor. Dr. Onika is the Founder and Director of Action Speaks Volume Orphanage Home and Sewing School in Telangana State, India, and the Founder and Director of Action Speaks Volume Sewing School in Khanewal and Shankot, Pakistan. She founded, operated, and visited an Orphanage home in Tuni, India, for four years, and she supported widows in Tuni, India.

She is the founder of Empowering Eight Inner Circle, ASV C.A.R.E.S, ASV Next Level Living Program, and P6 Solutions and Consulting. She has served for thirteen years as a therapeutic foster parent. Of all the things Dr. O does, she is most proud of her profound faith in Christ and her opportunity to serve the body of Christ globally.

Author's Website: *www.ActionSpeaksVolumes.com*

Book Series Website: *www.TheBookOfMentors.com*

> *"LEADERSHIP IS THE CHALLENGE TO BE SOMETHING MORE THAN AVERAGE."*
>
> ~ JIM ROHN

RITU CHOPRA
TIMELESS DILEMMAS— NAVIGATING YESTERDAY, TODAY, & TOMORROW

Humanity has always faced dilemmas that define its trajectory, whether in the past, present, or future. Yesterday's challenges often stemmed from survival and exploration of how to harness resources, build civilizations, and adapt to the unknown. These decisions shaped the frameworks of society but often left unresolved tensions that echo today.

In the present, dilemmas have evolved to balance tradition with progress. Questions of morality, technology, and sustainability dominate discussions, pushing individuals and societies to reconcile rapid innovation with enduring human values. Information is abundant, but clarity is elusive in an era of abundant information.

Tomorrow's dilemmas remain uncertain yet inevitable. How do we address the unintended consequences of today's choices? Can we create inclusive, ethical, and sustainable solutions?

This chapter explores these timeless dilemmas, connecting the threads of human experience across generations. In an ever-changing world, we are equipped to deal with complexities by leveraging lessons from the past.

Jim Rohn, a great mentor, renowned motivational speaker, and entrepreneur, emphasized personal development, discipline, and the power of consistent action. His teachings centered on the idea that Success is achieved through self-responsibility and deliberate effort.

Rohn believed that "you are the average of the five people you spend the most time with," highlighting the importance of surrounding oneself with positive influences. These timeless teachings are as valid today as they have been in the past.

Today, the 21st Century presents numerous challenges, but few stand out as particularly significant, and some align with the UN's Sustainable Goals closely:

1. Technological Disruption
2. Global Inequality (SDG#10)
3. Climate Change & Environmental Degradation (SDG#13)
4. Geopolitical Instability
5. Mental Health Crisis (SDG#3)

As the mentor, Jim Rohn, quoted, "Success is neither magical nor mysterious. Success is the natural consequence of consistently applying the basic fundamentals." It is up to us to use timeless teaching to help ourselves for our personal gain and the collective benefit of society.

Today's business philosophy focuses on profits and the bottom line. Each generation brings its own view of the world, which can be seen as opportunities and threats to businesses. This creates a great need to prepare each generation for the workforce a bit differently, especially in the era of high technology, Automation, and Artificial Intelligence.

What is needed, assessing the gaps, and how well we are equipped with today's tools and resources to shape our future. Management experts used to think that management decisions were purely secular and objective. They had no subjective cultural element involved when they made decisions regarding the company's management. A work culture's ethos and essence must be understood to make successful business decisions today since management is about motivating people.

The Industrial Revolutions mark transformative periods in human history, driven by technological advancements and their impact on society and the economy.

- 1st Industrial Revolution (18th - 19th Century)
- 2nd Industrial Revolution (Late 19th - Early 20th Century)
- 3rd Industrial Revolution (Mid-20th Century - Early 21st Century)
- 4th Industrial Revolution (21st Century)

Today's marketplace has crossed national boundaries into the invisible digital business landscape, and there is no going back. The lines between physical, digital, and biological spheres are blurring. Innovative systems enhance efficiency and raise ethical questions and challenges, like cybersecurity and job displacement. Each revolution has significantly altered how humans live and work, leading to progress but also requiring adaptation.

The industrial revolutions of the past Century have given us strong foundations, growth, and innovations to continue. Work ethics, business strategies, and innovation techniques of past generations following World War I and II created a foundation for our generation to expand and advance innovation in new industries.

At the beginning of the 21st Century, we live in a Global Village with integrated economies, information technology, and artificial intelligence being part of our daily lives. The rapid changes we have witnessed in the last two to three decades are mesmerizing. The rest of the 3rd decade will bring more changes rapidly with AI and Robotics - in our daily lives and work.

In business, how men and women communicate and interact has dramatically changed. During the past few decades, our roles, conversations, and expectations of each other have changed. But our disagreements, disconnect, and differences have remained, including the generational mindset. Instant messaging with abbreviated communications indicates our impulsiveness to respond, and the personal liability of self-development, as great masters have taught us, gets lost.

The personal touch in communications has been taken over by pictorial languages. As this is today's norm for exchanging our individual and business communications, we must find a way to bring timeless teaching to the new world of the 21st Century. We must understand the challenges, adapt to current behavior, support one another, and achieve measurable progress.

In the 21st Century, Rohn's principles remain profoundly relevant. The emphasis he places on adaptability and self-improvement equips individuals to deal with rapid technological advancements, economic uncertainty, and societal pressures. The discipline he advocated helps combat distractions in a digital age, while his emphasis on relationships resonates in building strong personal and professional networks. Rohn's teachings empower individuals to take control of their lives, fostering resilience and Success in an ever-evolving world.

In today's societies, Disparities in wealth, education, and healthcare remain pervasive, exacerbated by globalization and economic systems that often favor the affluent. These gaps fuel social unrest and limit collective progress. Conflicts, terrorism, and shifting power dynamics create global tensions. Cyber warfare, resource competition, and fragmented international cooperation further complicate diplomacy and peace-building.

Our personal journeys are on the cusp of fear, faith, and everything in between. We need not compete with others but try to overcome our own fears.

A Leadership Coach, Monte Pedersen, quotes, "From an execution perspective, we will always need head-driven leadership skills, and when we can add capabilities that provide trust, psychological safety, and emotional intelligence to balance, things get even better. While EQ has recently become one of the more dominant topics of discussion amongst leadership teams (and rightfully so), we can't forget about the operationally driven mindset and what it accomplishes in the workplace."

Leadership combines qualities that anyone can apply and lead others around them. We have seen young teenagers become leaders on the global stage, for example, Mallela Yosef, Greta Thunberg, and Boyan Slat. Leadership is not limited to specific corporate or organizational roles. These young people are perfect examples of leadership icons and beacons of hope.

A shared vision of humanity emphasizes the interconnectedness of all individuals, communities, and nations, grounded in mutual respect, empathy, and collective well-being. This vision promotes global cooperation, ethical behavior, and sustainable development to ensure equitable opportunities and dignity for everyone. Leadership is pivotal in shaping, nurturing, and realizing this shared vision.

Let's reflect upon how leadership aligns with a shared vision of humanity.

The shared vision for the future includes innovations in every field for the benefit of everyone and harmony with nature while integrating technology into our daily lives. We need to do our part to take the lead in making small changes for the future of our generations and the planet.

- Recognizing the intrinsic value of every individual, irrespective of race, gender, or socioeconomic status.
- Upholding global justice, equality, and human rights.
- Emphasizing sustainable living to preserve resources for future generations.
- Encouraging collaboration over competition to solve global challenges like poverty, climate change, and inequality.

Leaders are instrumental in translating a shared vision of humanity into actionable frameworks. We need leaders at every level in these societies, communities, and institutions of all sizes, not just in large organizations, for our sustainable earth, resources, and safe living conditions.

- Those who can craft and communicate a compelling vision that resonates with diverse audiences.

- Think beyond immediate gains to focus on human progress over the long term.

- Promote values-based leadership, focusing on integrity and ethics. Bridging divides by fostering dialogue and understanding.

- Building partnerships between nations, organizations, and communities to address global issues.

- Encouraging cross-cultural collaboration for innovation and problem-solving.

There were specific practices in many ancient cultures that rulers were taught and adhered to, which remain timeless advice for the leaders of any generation who are leading the organizations in our modern-day society. These values were founded by organizational leaders or leaders in any societal role to be mindful, compassionate, flexible, honest, and to serve with a sense of service to humanity.

We don't see that too often, yet the practices of today's leaders are seen to be self-interested or profit oriented. That does not mean these values have disappeared; they exist, and conscious leaders want to lead with them. Their honest and sincere interests in serving their consumers and prospects are influenced by the shareholder's values and become profit centric.

For a global village to care for our planet, our future, and the wellbeing of the earth's inhabitants, we must look at human strengths, resilience, and desire to take conscious action for humanity's future to create and raise conscious leaders of tomorrow. Leaders who champion corporate social responsibility (CSR) or fair governance and hold themselves and others responsible for decisions that impact humanity.

Leaders who embrace a shared vision of humanity inspire others to work together for a future that values dignity, fairness, and collective progress. In doing so, they become catalysts for creating a world where the wellbeing of humanity and the planet is the highest priority.

RITU CHOPRA

About Ritu Chopra: Ritu Chopra, a technologist by profession, an author, TV show host, award-winning film producer, a certified leadership coach, and international speaker who is on her spiritual journey.

With twenty five-plus years of experience in Fortune 500 companies serving in IT operations, information security in global financial, & health care industries, Ritu now mentors and coaches emerging leaders to achieve their "Personal Mastery."

Ritu is the Founder of Lead My Way, a not-for-profit organization, and she is a passionate advocate of women and youth leadership and empowerment initiatives.

Author Website: *www.RituChopra.com*

Book Series Website: *www.TheBookOfMentors.com*

SALLY WURR

PAY IT FORWARD—BECOME A MENTOR

Aspire to Inspire

Becoming a good mentor requires a commitment to continuous improvement and a genuine desire to help others grow and succeed. A combination of skills, qualities, and actions are required to guide and support someone in their personal or professional development. You may find yourself, like I did, becoming a mentor in a whole different environment than usual.

Being a great mentor is an ongoing process that requires dedication, self-awareness, and a commitment to your mentee's success and well-being. Your influence can have a profound impact on their personal and professional development, and by continually striving to improve your mentoring skills, you can make a significant difference in their lives.

The following is a list of traits of a great mentor:

- You must understand your role and responsibilities to your mentee. Recognize that your primary purpose is to support and guide the mentee's growth and development.

- You must build a strong relationship based on trust and rapport and be approachable, empathetic, and open-minded.

- It is important to set clear objectives. Sometimes, the mentee already has their objectives written out. You just need to work with them to make sure that your expertise and their goals will work well together.

- Provide constructive feedback but do so in a supportive and nonjudgmental manner. Encourage critical thinking and problem-solving rather than simply providing answers.

- Another important part of being a great mentor is to practice active listening by giving them your full attention. Ask open-ended questions to encourage them to express themselves.

- You need to recognize that growth and development take time, so be patient with setbacks and challenges.

- Adapt your mentoring approach to your mentee's unique needs and pace. Every mentee will go at a different speed. Be sure to match yours up with theirs; otherwise, your mentee could become overwhelmed with too much information.

- Introduce your mentee to relevant contacts in your industry or field. It helps them expand their professional network.

- In order to inspire your mentee, you need to acknowledge and celebrate their accomplishments, no matter how small. Positive reinforcement can boost their confidence and motivation as well as your own.

- Always maintain and respect the privacy of your mentee by keeping their personal and professional matters confidential unless they give explicit consent to share.

- A great mentor will also share relevant articles, books, and resources that can help in their development. Offer guidance on where to find additional learning opportunities. Above all, lead by example and demonstrate the qualities of behaviors you want your mentee to emulate. Be a role model in terms of professionalism, ethics, and morals.

A good mentor periodically assesses the relationship's progress. You discuss concerns or challenges and make adjustments as necessary. When the mentoring relationship concludes, discuss the progress made in the lessons learned. Help your mentee transition to the next stage of their development, whether it's independence or finding a new mentor.

As a mentor, you need to improve yourself continuously. Reflect on your own skills and seek to improve. Stay up to date with developments in your field.

Remember that being a good mentor is a two-way street. While you provide guidance and support, you can also learn from your mentees' experiences and perspectives. An effective mentoring relationship is mutually beneficial and fosters growth and development for both parties involved.

One way I have been able to grow in my role as a Mentor is by being a part of the Toastmasters International organization. Their curriculum teaches you speaking and leadership skills. The best role in a meeting is that of an Evaluator. As an evaluator, you listen to someone giving a verbal speech, and then you give them a verbal evaluation based on how they delivered the message of their speech. This role teaches critical thinking and listening skills and how to deliver specific feedback that can help them grow. You learn to give positive feedback and nestle in constructive criticism and additional options in a quick turnaround time.

As a bestselling, multi-book published author and Life Design Coach, I find myself mentoring people constantly. Mentoring does not have to be a long-term commitment. It can be a twenty-minute conversation about a specific topic or a six-week online class helping people develop their skills. Mentoring can fit many different situations.

After the loss of my husband to cancer in 2020, I have found myself in a special club. That of "widowhood." It has given me a unique opportunity to mentor other people who have suffered a loss. The loss of a family member is much different than that of a friend or associate.

Mentoring people who have lost a spouse or family member to death is a compassionate and essential role that can provide much-needed support during a difficult time.

Here are some key principles and strategies to consider when offering this type of mentoring:

- Offer immediate assistance and be there in person if possible. Sometimes, just having someone to sit with in silence can be comforting.

- Allow the grieving person to talk about their loved one and their feelings. Listen without judgment or interruption.

- Understand that grief has no set timeline. They may experience a range of emotions that can come and go in waves. Avoid rushing them to move on or get over it.

- Assist with organizing paperwork and legal matters, such as wills, estates, and insurance claims, if they ask you for assistance. Offer to handle daily tasks, like cooking meals, grocery shopping, or taking care of household chores.

- Encourage them to rely on their social network of friends and family. Offer to help coordinate visits or gatherings, providing companionship and comfort. If they express an interest in seeking help, attend support groups or therapy sessions with them.

- Understand that there will be times when they need solitude or time alone to process their feelings. Respect their need for space while reassuring them that you are available when they're ready to talk. Encourage them to reminisce and celebrate the life of their loved one, share stories, look at photos, and perhaps even create a scrapbook or a memorial in their honor.

- Provide practical support for the long term by continuing to check on them regularly.

- Remind them to take care of themselves physically and emotionally and to encourage regular exercise, proper nutrition, and adequate rest.

- Be mindful of special occasions by recognizing that holidays, anniversaries, and other special occasions can be difficult.

- Be sensitive to their cultural and religious beliefs and rituals related to death and the mourning period, and offer support that aligns with their values and practices.

Remember that everyone's grieving process is unique, and any support should be tailored to the individual's needs and preferences. Your presence and understanding can make a significant difference in helping them navigate the loss.

Being a mentor is a wonderfully rewarding role. It is truly a time to give back and Pay It Forward for all the times people have stepped up and helped you. Make a difference in the world around you.

SALLY WURR

About Sally Wurr: Sally Wurr is an international speaker and multi-book author.

Sally is known as the "Storm Whisperer" because her message is about how to prepare for life's storms. Each person has trials and tragedies, but it is how we react to those events that help us grow and survive in our business and personal activities.

By sharing her expertise with stories, she teaches you how to embrace change and how to face life's struggles head-on. Simply put, she likes to teach others how to problem solve.

Sally embraces the knowledge that those who can must be the ones that do. She shares her stories so that others can find their true purpose.

In addition to writing and speaking, Sally is the President and Founder of SW Insurance Corp. She has helped thousands of CEOs develop employee benefits programs to attain and retain employees. It is her problem-solving and attention to detail that have made her successful in this arena for many years.

Author's Website: *www.SallyWurr.com*

Book Series Website: *www.TheBookOfMentors.com*

"LEARN HOW TO BE HAPPY WITH WHAT YOU HAVE WHILE YOU PURSUE ALL THAT YOU WANT."

~ JIM ROHN

SARAH LEE

CAN YOU REALLY THINK & GROW RICH? JIM DID!

. . . .

I talk about *Think and Grow Rich* a lot. I think about it a lot, too.

I teach it to many, chapter by chapter, in my International Think and Grow Rich Book Club, which I founded and run weekly for fans of TRG.

The largest classes I have held so far have had 250-300 students a week, showing up to learn from me remotely during COVID.

Some context, if you please. I have worked with John Shin weekly as a boss and mentor for the last fourteen years. He is one of my business partners for one of my companies. John owns a percentage of my current Financial Services Agency. John is a great mentor, master communicator, and the Executive Producer of the movie, *Think and Grow Rich: The Legacy*. We both are very experienced in business and in coaching.

When we come across a new student, one who says they want to make a change, I love it. They want more happiness, more freedom, more resources, and more respect to know they and their loved ones will be taken care of financially in the future. They want a different result, to which I hear, "I want to be different."

I used to think that was self-evident. I used to think that all people knew that to get a different result, they had to think about different things and think differently from how they think now. I used to think that everyone knew this.

Experience is what taught me the nuances of what that really was. Over the last twenty-plus years, I have learned that many of them want the result or the feeling but do not want to do the work, take the risk, or change their outlook enough to "get there." Wherever "there" is for them.

It is why people like me, who know the exact steps of how to help people evolve and achieve (read: get the results they are seeking), often work in professional settings and not as coaches or consultants. Often, coaches will guide you, support you, or even hold you accountable, but often, they do not have the experience, tools, and ability (read: resources and tools) needed to help you get there yourself.

Consultants have the tools, but Professionals have clients who come to them knowing they have a problem. It's best to be a Professional, then a Consultant, and at least a Coach. Coaches are at a disadvantage because the clients they could serve the best often do not want to do the work and often do not even know there is a solution to their problem—or even what their problem is.

So, when someone comes to John or me, we tend to focus on three things in my "day job:" financial education and literacy, business coaching, and agency leadership development. We teach you what to do with money, how to earn it, save it, multiply it, and build upon it. This starts with your mind and mindset.

You cannot run a business without knowing and doing the things you need to do to run a business. Many people are interested in "having more, being more and doing more" but many of those people are not interested in "doing what it takes to become the person who can do the thing that leads to the result." That is unfortunate.

In the book, *Think and Grow Rich*, we talk about building things from Desire. Desire has a value and purpose. If you are an artist, a creator of any kind, you build from Desire. You build because you have to. You need to see the thing that you have in your mind so you can show it to other people. That is called enrollment.

Business is the same. If you want a business that grows, you must love your product. Love who you serve, and love to see people change or their circumstances change as a result of using what you created or invented. A business must serve a purpose or a need or it will not grow.

A business must have processes, or it will never become systematic. If there are no systems, there is no expansion. No expansion means not enough people will be able to benefit from it and exchange money for the value you bring.

In my *Think and Grow Rich* class, I am often caught saying that all real businesses or income streams need to start from Desire, not need. If you need money, get a job. If you want to solve a problem, start a business.

So, Desire has immense value in business, in growth, and in creation.

But Jim Rohn said, "Without a sense of urgency, desire loses its value."

Sarah Principle: We cannot just "want something different"—we must take action to create something different.

Jim Rohn also said, "How sad to see a father (a person) with money and no joy. The man studied economics but never studied happiness."

Sarah Principle: If you only learn the technical aspects of money, then money does not serve you and thus does not serve its purpose.

Money is there to serve you and to serve your ability to serve others. It is a tool, an energy, and an extension of you.

Money is not to be hoarded; it is there to circulate. It is there to serve, to do its job for the "many, not the few." Money wants to be taken care of. It wants to serve its purpose; if you mismanage it, it will leave you and go to someone else who knows what to do with it. Making you happy is one of its jobs—but not its only job.

"You can change yourself. You are not a tree you can't move. You are not a goose. You can decide your direction."
~ Jim Rohn

Sarah Principle: When you change your mind, you will change your life.

Change comes from mindset first and then shows up in 3D reality later. Your thoughts create your actions, and your actions are evidence to others of who you are, what you want, and what you deserve and will put up with.

What people who focus on manifestation forget is that to get what you want, you need to become the person who can do the thing you want to do. Earl Nightingale said that best.

"If the why is powerful, the how is easy."
~ Jim Rohn

Sarah Principle: People do not care what you do; they care what you can do for them. They pay for results and solutions, not the process —unless the process works well and is easy, then they pay you for the process to "get to the result."

This is the same as, "People don't care what you do until they know how much you care."

"Life is both sugar and strychnine, you got to be careful what you ingest."
~ Jim Rohn

"You develop your skills and personality in private, so it serves you in front of thousands. Practice well when no one is watching."
~ Jim Rohn

Sarah Principal: This is one of the hardest parts of growth, as a famous football player said, "No one is watching, but keep making plays."

Business success comes in part from momentum. You have to keep motivating yourself until others can see your vision, and until you are discovered by your champion. Sometimes, that champion is you and the people you serve.

> *"Excuses are the nails used to build a house of failure."*
> ~ Jim Rohn

Sarah Principle: "I don't take excuses; I don't give excuses. If you want something or are something, stand on it. Don't allow people to bully you with their "opinions"—make them prove it.

We all have our opinions, but success leaves clues, and *Think and Grow Rich* left us a roadmap.

There is no need to reinvent the wheel when someone has kindly already written the outline for success.

If you are right, it will show up; if you are wrong, and you keep an open mind, you will learn. Either way, it is part of success.

Jim Rohn was a master teacher on the thought process of change and change management. He called it leadership and leadership development, which is what John and I call it, but Jim Rohn left us the clues for those who came afterward, clues so we could copy him and learn from his mastery of the subject of growth mindset and achievement.

He is one of the heroes of mindset teaching. He is one of my favorites to incorporate into my courses and teachings because, while you cannot do it for them, you can show people the way and encourage them to take the steps toward their own future.

Thoughts are things. We change first with our mindset and knowledge, then with our application and testing of that knowledge, and those tests lead to changes in our behavior and circumstances.

I will leave you with this thought.

I have worked in event production for Tony Robbins for over ten years now. Tony's first and best mentor was Jim Rohn. Tony taught me so much about coaching, events, mindset, delivery, and business.

This is what he said about Jim:

"My original teacher was a man named Jim Rohn, an Idaho farm boy and Sears clerk who made it big as a motivational speaker and author. He held seminars all across the country for forty years. He was a millionaire by the age of thirty-one and authored seventeen books."

Without Jim, there would have been no Tony Robbins, and Tony is considered the most prolific coach and speaker of our time. He's a living legend and a huge influence on me, both personally and professionally.

Without Tony Robbins, I would never have been a coach, mindset trainer, host, or motivational speaker. So, I owe a lot to Jim Rohn, a man I never met but have been a huge fan of for years. He has influenced me from beyond the grave.

When John Shin first asked to mentor me, he asked me to sell my financial services business, where I had multiple Allstate Agency offices and their clients as my primary clients, and come follow him in business.

The second thing he said was, "I only want to mentor people who want to leave a legacy. Do you want to leave a legacy? What do you want it to be?" At that time, I just wanted to make more money. $200,000 a year was not enough money to achieve my dreams in San Francisco. I was not getting ahead fast enough, I thought.

So I said, "No, not yet." That changed our relationship ever so slightly.

Now, and for the last many years, I have been able to say I have been putting my all into my Legacy. I know who I am now, what I do well, who I want to affect and impact, and how I wish to be remembered when I am gone.

Legacy is powerful. Jim Rohn left one—this book is part of it. Go out and create yours today!

SARAH LEE

About Sarah Lee, MBA: A brilliant educational psychologist and leadership expert by education, Sarah Lee is the innovative author of *Rock Soup - An Innovational Idea in Leadership.* By profession, Sarah has been teaching financial literacy for the last fifteen years using her own firm as a platform. She is a full-service financial advisor and manager of her own Securities Branch of a national firm. She has networked with 100 Brokers all over the US. Sarah has an MBA in Finance and Social Impact and is fourteen months shy of a Ph.D. in Educational Leadership. She is also the founder of multiple other companies and brands; some sold for profit, some she learned from, and some she consulted on for other businesses. She is now mostly currently focused on her production company with her husband, MONEY MENTOR, LLC™.

She has been advocating and speaking on large issues like financial literacy, literacy mindset, clean water, and service to the world (hunger, water issues, poverty, and literacy) for her entire life. At nine-years-old, she said, "I would like to host a consumer reports show, where I would interview local business owners and see how I could highlight them while giving them ways to give back and make a difference." That led to a life of public speaking, running endowments, and working with local universities on educational issues. She developed her world-famous business philosophy during this time: "Business is just like Rock Soup…" @coachmeSarahLee, @moneymentormethod; Instagram: @moneymentorcompany, @coachmeacademy. For Money Tips, you can text the words "MONEYMENTOR" to 55444 for a free gift or visit our webpage: linktr.ee/MoneyMentorMethod.

Author's Website: *www.MoneyMentorFreeGift.com*

Book Series Website: *www.TheBookOfMentors.com*

"DISCIPLINE IS THE BRIDGE BETWEEN GOALS AND ACCOMPLISHMENT."

~ JIM ROHN

STACEY HALL

THE WAVES OF MENTORSHIP

Mentorship is a journey that generates far-reaching impacts, influencing lives well beyond one's immediate circle. I've learned so many lessons through growth, resilience, and empowerment. Each mentoring relationship has unique dynamics, yet they all share the common goal of fostering growth and understanding. I'm filled with gratitude for the mentors who've guided me and the mentees who have trusted me. Together, we create shared experiences and wisdom, creating waves that speak to the enduring strength of human connection.

In the spirit of mentorship, I am reminded that its true power lies in its ability to transcend boundaries, cultures, and generations. It is a force that uplifts communities, nurtures dreams, and inspires us to reach our highest potential. Whether through a simple word of encouragement, thoughtful advice, or a shared moment of vulnerability, mentorship changes lives in profound and lasting ways.

As we continue to navigate our personal and professional journeys, let us embrace the role of both mentor and mentee. Let us commit to nurturing a culture of mentorship that champions empathy, understanding, and hope. By doing so, we honor those who have guided us and paved the way for future leaders, dreamers, and change-makers who will carry the torch forward.

Growing up, I experienced mentorship in many forms. Although my parents believed in me and instilled in me the values of hard work and perseverance, my faith journey was one of self-discovery and personal experience. These weren't just lessons for survival; they were principles for thriving. My mother's support in me and my father's tireless work ethic laid a foundation for my life.

Throughout my professional journey, mentorship has taken on greater significance for me. At Virginia Tech and later at VCU's MCV School of Dentistry, I encountered mentors who taught me that dentistry is not just about repairing teeth but treating the whole person. These mentors emphasized the importance of empathy and understanding lessons that have stayed with me throughout my career.

Establishing the Williamsburg Center for Dental Health in 2011 was a leap of faith, but it also reflected the valuable mentorship I received along the way. My mentors instilled in me the confidence to pursue my vision and provided me with the necessary tools to turn it into reality. Today, my practice is more than just a workplace; it's a community where mentorship flourishes. I have established an environment and culture of mentorship where mentoring happens daily. I have mentored so many people over the year, instilling our core values of "Always Learning." Whether I'm helping my team master new techniques or educating patients about their oral health, mentorship lies at the core of everything we do.

It's a place where every interaction is an opportunity for growth, learning, and mutual respect. The center has become a nurturing environment where staff and patients feel supported and empowered. This culture of mentorship has not only enhanced our professional skills but has also fostered a sense of belonging and purpose.

By prioritizing education and communication, we empower our patients to participate actively in their oral health journey. Looking ahead, I am excited about expanding our support through our practice and exploring new ways to positively impact our community. Our goal is to extend the benefits of mentorship beyond the walls of our practice. Doing so, I aim to inspire my immediate influence on dental professionals and contribute to a healthier, more informed community. Every interaction with a patient presents an opportunity to educate, empower, and build trust. I've had patients express their gratitude for the dental care they received and the kindness and respect they experienced in my practice. One patient remarked that they felt "heard and valued," which perfectly captures the essence of mentorship—guiding others with empathy and understanding.

In essence, the Williamsburg Center for Dental Health results from positive mentorship—a living example of how guidance, support, and shared knowledge can transform lives and communities for the better. From hosting monthly drives for community-based needs to keeping our dental office and practice open to the public, we always seek to educate, inform, and keep our community happy and healthy.

One of the most profound aspects of mentorship is its reciprocity. While I have mentored many individuals, I have also learned invaluable lessons from my mentees. For instance, a young dental assistant gave me innovative ideas to improve patient flow. Her fresh perspective reminded me of the importance of remaining open to learning, regardless of position or experience level.

My mentorship style and approach extend beyond the confines of my community and practice. My mission work in Honduras and El Salvador with Orphan Helpers has been a humbling reminder of the universal need for guidance and support. Many children I've worked with have faced unimaginable hardships, yet their resilience is a testament to the power of mentorship and faith. I took a young mentee to a course for free; she audited the course learning and observing. As a result of her learning, she took the initiative to cross borders to bring everything she learned about education and inclusion. She has since returned to Honduras and improved the dental industry there, perpetuating the wave of mentorship and faithful serving of those in need. These experiences have reinforced my belief that mentorship is about imparting knowledge and instilling hope in everyone.

Beyond the borders of philanthropy, this relationship with trust, faith, and belief has influenced my relationships. One of my co-workers has since retired. Although she and I were colleagues throughout our careers, she and I have become lifelong friends, accountability partners, and bible study partners. The crucial years of working together and building our practice have now developed an even deeper relationship—Coffee with Carolyn, I call it. Now, I am an accountability partner, which has been even more impactful than our professional working relationship over the years.

Faith has always been my anchor, guiding me through life's challenges and triumphs. As a mentor figure to others, my faith inspires me to lead with compassion and integrity. It reminds me that mentorship is a calling —an opportunity to make a meaningful impact on others' lives. This belief was particularly poignant during one of the most challenging periods of my life: navigating a divorce while managing my practice and raising my daughters. In those moments, I leaned heavily on my faith and the lessons imparted by my mentors. Their guidance and unwavering support helped me find strength and clarity.

Motherhood has been one of my life's most rewarding and experiential mentorship roles. Raising my three daughters has taught me more about resilience, love, and leadership than any professional experience ever could. My kids are so different, which has only enhanced the experience of providing for, educating, and trusting in their growth. I am an advocate for raising independent women. I have friends who struggle to navigate raising their kids and then letting them board planes and leave the house. My girls have the travel sense and capability to travel internationally with ease. Independence contributes to confidence and self-sustainability, and now they will even eat anything I cook—which is a brave adventurer for all hungry hearts. Watching them grow into strong, independent young women fills me with immense pride and joy. Through this journey, I have learned that mentorship is not about creating replicas of ourselves but empowering others to become their best versions.

One of my proudest moments as a mentor was when a former mentee shared how our conversations inspired her to pursue her dream of opening her practice. Her success story reminded me that mentorship involves planting seeds, even if we don't always immediately see the results of our efforts.

I've discovered mentorship opportunities within the broader dental community that continually shape my development. Being part of the Implant Study Club has been a cornerstone of my professional growth.

This group of like-minded professionals offers a space for vulnerability, learning, and mutual support. Through our shared experiences, I've recognized the importance of community in mentorship. It reminds us that we are stronger together and that collaboration often leads to the most profound insights. It's like that old adage, "If you are the smartest person in the room, then you are in the wrong room."

As I look to my future as a person and professional, I am dedicated to broadening the positive impact of mentorship with my immediate scope of practice and influence. I extend this vision and mission to the kids and community by providing opportunities to learn and see how this profession operates—building genuine interest and education for young and older people. Through professional practice, community service, and mentoring my daughters, I aim to foster an environment where others can flourish.

Mentorship is a valuable gift that continually provides benefits to both parties. It represents a journey of mutual growth, showcasing the impact of belief in one another. This relationship creates a legacy that we can all contribute to. Let us strive to be both mentors and mentees, fostering waves of positive change that will resonate for generations to come.

STACEY HALL

About Dr. Stacey Hall: Dr. Stacey Hall, DDS brings her unique outlook on dental care and her personable optimism to the Williamsburg Center for Dental Health. After nine years of solid dental expertise as a dentist in Williamsburg, she then decided in early 2011 to branch out and open her own local practice, Williamsburg Center for Dental Health.

After completing her degrees from Virginia Tech in 1998, Dr. Hall graduated from VCU's MCV School of Dentistry in 2002, receiving her D.D.S. She is a member of the American Academy of Cosmetic Dentistry, Academy of General Dentistry, the American Dental Association, and was awarded member fellowship to the International Congress of Oral Implantology in 2008. Dr. Hall is a scholar with the internationally renowned Dawson Academy.

She is part-time faculty with the Academy, assistant teaching for courses concerning occlusion and rehabilitation of worn dentition. Dr. Hall also leads their ambassador program. Stacey has been blessed with three beautiful daughters, Lanie, Gracie, and Abbie. One attends the University of Tampa, and the other two are very active in high school. She is a loyal Virginia Tech Football fan and enjoys being on the water on her boat, relaxing at her river house, paddle boarding (even with her dog), skiing, Bible study, and missions work.

Author's Website: *www.WilliamsburgDentalHealth.com*

Book Series Website: *www.TheBookOfMentors.com*

STEPH SHINABERY

MENTORSHIP IN AN EVOLVING WORLD

Mentorship has long been essential in my personal and professional lives; yet, as I navigate this journey, I realize its evolution. Where once mentors served solely as sources of advice to their mentees, mentoring is increasingly shifting into dynamic reciprocal relationships that benefit both parties involved.

Looking back over my mentors—Steve, my aunt, and my high school basketball coach—I see they shared qualities like authenticity, vulnerability, and genuine connections, which I consider even more critical given today's rapidly morphing world!

In previous chapters in this series, I have described mentors who saw something special in me but couldn't see for myself, investing their time, energy, and wisdom to facilitate my growth. Over time, however, as my experience deepened, I became acutely aware that mentorship involved guidance, alignment, authenticity, and mutual growth. Therefore, in this chapter of my mentorship journey, I investigate its changing form today and its effect on me.

Mentorship is Focused on Authenticity

One of the defining trends of modern mentorship is an increased emphasis on authenticity. While social media and digital communications may lead to superficial interactions, authentic mentoring provides real and meaningful relationships. Being true to yourself—accepting strengths and weaknesses while encouraging others to do likewise—and inviting all parties involved (mentoring participants and mentors) into fully participatory interactions that encourage mutuality between one person and another is what people value most in mentorship relationships! It takes presence for mentoring relationships!

Being authentic means recognizing our freedom from society or past experiences that put roles or expectations upon us. Breaking free is the cornerstone of success in mentorship relationships!

My journey to authenticity has not always been easy; at times, expressing myself freely without fearing judgment or rejection was difficult. With mentors' guidance and example as my guideposts, I learned the power of being true to oneself to create impactful mentorship relationships. By being authentic individuals, we create an atmosphere where others feel safe expressing themselves freely without judgment from outside sources. Mutual authenticity forms lasting bonds beyond traditional mentorship relationships.

Acceptance of Mentor-Mentee Align

Modern mentorship has evolved with an increased emphasis on alignment. In the past, mentorship often consisted of authoritarian arrangements wherein experts taught their protégées their craft; modern mentoring seeks to build partnerships based upon shared values, goals, and visions, which helps ensure both professionally and personally beneficial relationships are fostered between mentors and protégées.

My relationship with Steve taught me the power of alignment. Not only was he a professional advice provider, but we also established win-win situations where both parties gained equally from our shared growth over time.

Genius Code Academy highlights the value of mentorship that aligns with one's values and personal journey. Aligning with one's values can create synergies that facilitate growth while expanding horizons for discovery.

Modern Mentorship Takes on its Reciprocal Form

Today's mentorship has undergone significant changes to make it into what it is today. It is no longer an unbalanced trust; instead, it operates like a two-way street where both parties learn, grow, and benefit equally. This mutuality makes mentorship an impactful form of relationship building; exchanging experiences can enrich both sides.

Mentorship has taught me as much from my mentees as it has from me. Their fresh perspectives, creative ideas, and energetic enthusiasm inspired and challenged my thinking about bringing about change! Mutual learning makes mentorship such an enjoyable experience—it's not simply imparting knowledge; mentorship means growing together!

A friend came to me with an outstanding project idea that perfectly aligned with Genius Code Academy values, yet, as I worked together with her, I soon discovered I was learning just as much from her as from me—her enthusiasm and creativity inspired my approach to work more meaningfully and gave me a renewed sense of purpose. This experience reinforced once again that mentorship should be seen as mutually beneficial, with both parties having something valuable to contribute.

Living Authentically: Responsibilities of Mentors

As mentors, we must live lives that reflect who we are. Our mentees rely on us not just for advice but as role models when faced with life's obstacles and difficulties. Being authentic means accepting ourselves even when that may prove challenging. Being open about struggles or vulnerabilities while teaching students that it's okay to make mistakes is a hallmark of authentic mentors.

One of the key lessons I have learned as a mentor is that authenticity breeds authenticity. By showing up as authentic versions of ourselves, we create an environment in which others feel safe expressing themselves openly as well, forging stronger ties between students and mentors that exceed traditional mentoring and building stronger bonds of mutual respect, trust, and growth for both parties involved.

Harnessing Vulnerability in Mentorship as a Competitive Edge

Vulnerability is another integral aspect of modern mentorship, although once considered undesirable. Gone are the days when mentors were seen as unwavering figures who always knew all the answers; now, vulnerability is seen as an asset. Creating safe spaces where mentors are willing to show weakness allows mentees the freedom and space they need for personal expression and growth.

As part of my mentorship journey, I've come to recognize that the power of vulnerability is not weakness—instead, it provides a remarkable platform for connection and growth. Sharing struggles and challenges helps mentees see they're not alone on their journey while opening up more about themselves fully, creating deeper bonds of friendship, mutual respect, and greater mutual understanding between us all.

Mentorship to Help Achieve Digital Era Success

Digital innovation has revolutionized how we view mentoring. While traditional face-to-face mentoring remains highly beneficial, digital communications channels now enable new forms of connecting across continents, time zones, and cultural borders thanks to technological innovations like Zoom.

Digital mentorship has enabled me to expand my reach, connecting with individuals who share my values and vision. Thanks to online platforms, I've mentored individuals all around the globe by helping unlock their potential and achieve their goals; this digital approach to mentorship has broadened my scope while broadening my perspective from different experiences and viewpoints.

Digital mentorship presents its own distinct challenges. Forming authentic, meaningful connections may prove more challenging when communication occurs solely via text and video calls, making establishing lasting mentorship relationships in this space challenging. To address these hurdles, I strive to develop intentional interactions between myself and my mentees—through personalized messages, virtual workshops, or one-on-one video sessions—prioritizing authenticity and vulnerability as part of creating powerful digital mentoring relationships that transcend virtual borders.

Next Steps in Mentorship

Mentorship's most rewarding aspects lie in its potential to have an immense ripple effect far beyond any single relationship. When we invest in others, they, in turn, become mentors themselves—spreading the knowledge, wisdom, and support they've received into communities across society, creating growth through empowerment and positive transformation. Mentoring leaves a legacy of growth behind it all.

At Genius Code Academy, I've witnessed this transformation firsthand. Many of my mentees use the tools and insights acquired to assist others on their journeys, truly showing its transformative powers that extend far beyond individual aid to create positive change throughout society! Mentorship truly has incredible transforming potential!

By living authentically, accepting vulnerability, and cultivating alignment, we can leave behind an impactful legacy of mentorship to empower future generations.

Continue the Mentorship Revolution

As my mentorship journey unfolds, I am more committed than ever to embracing modern mentorship principles and revolution. Mentorship goes well beyond simply offering advice: it requires building authentic connections between mentors and mentees, encouraging mutual growth, and leaving an indelible mark on society overall. Mentorship allows us to live our truth while helping empower others on their path toward empowerment.

Our Journey Begins Once More

Mentorship is not an endpoint but a journey toward continuous personal and professional development. Mentors journey alongside their mentees on this path together, providing support during highs and lows, successes or challenges encountered along the way, and moments of clarity or confusion experienced along this journey. A journey such as this requires openness, curiosity, and dedication toward our own development and those we mentor.

As I've explored mentorship further, I have come to recognize its greatest effectiveness when we show up fully, authentically, and vulnerable. Acknowledging our imperfections and sharing stories that ring true for others—creating space where everyone feels seen, heard, and valued. True transformation can happen when relationships go beyond superficial surface levels to inspire people to discover their inner power and take steps toward realizing it.

Mentorship is about passing on what we learn to others, leaving an impactful legacy for communities, industries, and societies as a whole.

I encourage you to embrace the mentorship revolution in your own life. Seek mentors whose values and vision align with yours or become mentors yourself for others. Live authentically while giving freely; together, we can transform mentorship into a powerful force for positive change!

STEPH SHINABERY

About Steph Shinabery: Steph Shinabery is The World's Best Possibility Coach, and a Nurse Anesthesiologist, Artist, Speaker, and the Founder of GENIUS CODE ACADEMY.

After spending much of her life in a career that lacked the inspiration and fulfillment she knew was available to her, she began a journey to answer the question: "What is it I truly desire?"

Her journey led to the creation of the Genius Identity Code™, a process for unlocking your gift, purpose and path, and helping people see, believe and execute their unique genius to achieve miraculous outcomes.

Steph works with creative experts, entrepreneurs and coaches to help them embrace their authenticity and create a life that gets them excited to jump out of bed every day!

You can find her talk, "Wake Up Your Genius Machine," on Amazon Prime Video's *Speak Up: Empower Your Ideas, Season 4*.

Author's Website: *www.StephShinabery.com* & *www.GeniusCodeAcademy.com*

Book Series Website: *www.TheBookOfMentors.com*

TAYLOR L. COLE

MENTORING, DISCIPLINE, & THE ROLE OF HABITS

What's Your Motivation?

Starting something new, whether it's a goal, project, spiritual discipline, or mentoring relationship, often feels daunting. Jim Rohn once said, "Motivation is what gets you started. Habit is what keeps you going." This insight speaks directly to why many people struggle to begin or maintain spiritual practices—they rely on bursts of motivation instead of building consistent habits.

Motivation can spark the desire to lose weight, learn a new skill, start dating again, pray, read scripture, or fast, but it's the development of habits that carries us through when enthusiasm wanes.

For instance, I've found that starting my day with prayer and scripture reading has become a habit that grounds me. Even on days when I feel distracted or unmotivated, this practice helps me begin the day with a sense of peace and direction, knowing that God is with me. Over time, the habit itself becomes the fuel that keeps me connected to God.

As mentors, we have the opportunity to encourage those we guide to take the first step—whether it's setting aside five minutes for prayer or reflecting on a single scripture. By helping them create small, manageable habits, we equip them with tools to sustain their spiritual growth long after the initial motivation fades. Just as Rohn emphasized

271

the importance of habits in achieving goals, spiritual disciplines enable us to stay connected to Jesus and grow into the people God has called us to be.

Over the course of a year, I studied twelve spiritual habits. I learned that these were not rules to follow or mandates but invitations to do things a different way. Instead of letting the world, social media, pop culture, or my own selfish desires guide me, I could allow the life of Jesus to be my best example and be mentored by Him.

Here are the spiritual disciplines.

1. Reading Scripture

"Your word is a lamp to my feet and a light to my path."
~ Psalm 119:105

Immersing ourselves in God's Word allows us to know His heart and receive His guidance. Regular scripture reading builds wisdom, deepens faith, and equips us to mentor others with truth.

2. Meditation

"Blessed is the one... whose delight is in the law of the Lord, and who meditates on His law day and night."
~ Psalm 1:1-2

Meditation invites us to dwell on God's Word, internalizing His truth and allowing it to shape our thoughts and actions.

For a long time, I was accustomed to memorizing scripture and could recite verses from memory with ease. However, I came to realize that I wasn't truly allowing those verses to shape my thoughts or influence my perspective in meaningful ways.

Through the discipline of meditation, I began to slow down and focus not just on the words but on their implications for my life. For example, as I memorized John 15:1-17, I took time to meditate on what it means to "abide in Christ" and bear fruit. This practice helped me see how God was calling me to apply these truths in my relationships and leadership. Meditation is more than memorization—it's letting scripture settle deep into your heart and transform your mind.

3. Celebration

> *"Rejoice in the Lord always; again I will say, rejoice."*
> ~ Philippians 4:4

Celebration reminds us to thank God for His blessings, building a spirit of gratitude and joy. It strengthens community bonds and shifts our focus from trials to God's faithfulness.

4. Prayer

> *"Pray without ceasing."*
> ~ 1 Thessalonians 5:17

Prayer is a direct line of communication with God, offering praise, seeking guidance, and interceding for others. It is foundational to our relationship with Him and a powerful tool in mentoring others.

5. Fasting

> *"When you fast, do not look somber as the hypocrites do… But when you fast, put oil on your head and wash your face."*
> ~ Matthew 6:16-17

Fasting focuses our hearts on God, teaching reliance on Him and creating space to hear His voice more clearly. It's omitting something of significance to make more room for Jesus.

6. Sabbath

> *"The Sabbath was made for mankind, not mankind for the Sabbath."*
> ~ Mark 2:27

Observing Sabbath rest reminds us to trust God's provision, step away from busyness, and find renewal in His presence.

7. Silence & Solitude

"But Jesus often withdrew to lonely places and prayed."
~ Luke 5:16

Taking time for silence and solitude allows us to disconnect from distractions and refocus on God's voice and will.

Initially, I thought silence and solitude simply meant being alone—separating myself from noise and busyness for a while. Although that's certainly part of it, I've learned it's much more than just physical isolation. Silence and solitude have become an opportunity to dream with God about the life we're living together.

It's in these quiet moments that I ask God to show me where He's leading me, what He desires for my relationships, and how He wants me to grow. These times of stillness have become a place of collaboration with God, where I can set aside my own plans and align my heart with His.

8. Simplicity

"Do not store up for yourselves treasures on earth... but store up for yourselves treasures in heaven."
~ Matthew 6:19-20

Living simply shifts our focus from material possessions to eternal priorities, helping us mentor others with an eternal perspective. Simplicity can also mean reducing obligations and learning to say no to some things so you can say yes to the right things.

9. Community

"And let us consider how to stir up one another to love and good works,
not neglecting to meet together."
~ Hebrews 10:24-25

Community provides support, accountability, and encouragement as we pursue God's purposes together.

Community has been a rich source of growth for me. It's not just about having people around—it's about learning from and sharing with others.

In my own journey, I've found that being part of a small group or ministry team offers unique opportunities to see how God is working in the lives of others. Their stories inspire me, and their insights often challenge me to think differently or step outside of my comfort zone.

Community also provides a space to share my experiences and encourage others in their walk with God. It's a two-way relationship that sharpens and strengthens everyone involved, as Proverbs 27:17 reminds us: "Iron sharpens iron, and one person sharpens another."

10. Service

"Just as the Son of Man did not come to be served, but to serve."
~ Matthew 20:28

Serving others reflects Christ's love and humility. Mentoring involves modeling a servant-hearted approach to leadership.

11. Generosity

"It is more blessed to give than to receive." .
~ Acts 20:35

Generosity cultivates a heart of selflessness, mirroring God's abundant provision.

12. Confession & Repentance

"If we confess our sins, He is faithful and just to forgive us our sins and to cleanse us from all unrighteousness."
~ 1 John 1:9

Confession restores our relationship with God and others, encouraging honesty and humility in mentoring relationships.

Engaging in these spiritual disciplines fosters personal growth and equips us to mentor others effectively. Habits like prayer, scripture reading, and generosity create space for God to transform us from the inside out. This transformation impacts how we lead and mentor others by helping us guide with wisdom, empathy, and humility.

These disciplines also provide a foundation for receiving insight and encouragement with a teachable heart when we are mentored by others. True, lasting success comes not from what we achieve on our own but from cultivating God's character in ourselves and others. By practicing these disciplines, we invite others to experience the abundant life that comes from walking closely with Christ.

Key Takeaways

1. Small Steps Lead to Big Growth: Begin with manageable habits like five minutes of prayer or a single verse of scripture. Small, consistent actions create lasting change.

2. Discipline Bridges the Gap: As Jim Rohn said, "Discipline is the bridge between goals and accomplishment." Spiritual disciplines bridge the gap between our desire for closeness with God and the transformation He desires to work in us.

3. Mentors Multiply Growth: Sharing your journey with a mentor or mentee deepens the impact of spiritual disciplines. Relationships are key to sustaining and growing in faith.

4. Remember the Invitation: Spiritual disciplines are not burdens or mandates—they are invitations to live as Jesus did and experience His peace, joy, and freedom.

What's your next step? Are you ready to confidently embrace spiritual disciplines as you mentor?

TLC

TAYLOR L. COLE

About Taylor L. Cole: Taylor L. Cole is a seasoned professional dedicated to helping meaningful brands capture the attention they deserve. With a career spanning over fourteen years, Taylor has honed her skills in Communications, PR, and social media, working with Fortune 500 companies, multi-national corporations, and startups across various industries including travel, tech, healthcare, and consumer products. Starting her journey in the world of television while still in high school, Taylor quickly made her mark, producing her first major show as an undergraduate at Southern Methodist University. She has since taken on leadership roles in communications and public relations at renowned companies such as Kimberly Clark, Hotels.com, Expedia, and Sabre.

As a guide for brands and leaders, Taylor specializes in crafting effective messaging and on-camera strategies, featuring her clients on quality, international TV programs and podcasts. She is the executive producer and host of *The Focus* and *Speak Up* on Amazon Prime Video, as well as the travel TV show *Hotel Hunt*, where she explores stunning destinations and uncovers unique accommodations. Her latest project is *Workable Faith*, a show where she engages with business leaders about integrating faith into the marketplace.

Taylor is also a dedicated community member, serving on various non-profit boards, business leadership groups, and actively participating in her church. Her involvement includes roles with the American Diabetes Association, Fellowship Power Lunch, Truth at Work, Valley Creek Church, and SMU.

Author's Website: *www.TVWithTLC.com*

Book Series Website: *www.TheBookOfMentors.com*

"SUCCESS IS ATTRACTED BY THE PERSON YOU BECOME."

~ JIM ROHN

VIKKI ROOD

THE GIFT OF GIVING BACK

In my lifetime, I've encountered countless mixed messages. Society expects us to be there for everyone in our lives while simultaneously emphasizing the importance of self-care—physically, emotionally, and spiritually. We're told to work tirelessly, arrive early, assert ourselves as leaders, and excel as parents. Simultaneously, we're warned not to be too assertive, yet encouraged to speak our truth. These messages are not only confusing but also conflicting, often presenting standards that feel impossible to meet.

What if, instead, we embraced a simpler approach? What if we allowed ourselves to slow down and simply do our best? Sometimes, my best involves achieving significant success at work. Other times, it means recognizing that my best effort for the day is taking time to rest and recharge.

In the journey of life, each of us navigates a path of self-discovery, gradually unraveling the layers to reveal our authentic selves. There are no certainties, no guarantees etched in stone, despite the pervasive messages suggesting otherwise. My personal odyssey has taught me a profound truth: I am ultimately responsible for my own journey. The tapestry of my achievements, emotions, and experiences has woven together the person I am today.

For many years, my self-worth was entangled with the external validations sought from family, coworkers, lovers, and even strangers. I lived in the shadow of others' expectations, believing that their acceptance defined my worth.

As I matured, I realized that the journey is solitary, inherently mine to walk. Embracing this truth liberated me, allowing me to approach each day with greater ease and joy. Wayne Dyer taught that they have resonated deeply with me with their direct simplicity. His words on love, in particular, have transformed my understanding of relationships.

I must confess, however, that this mindset didn't come naturally to me, especially in intimate relationships. I once erected boundaries and administered unconscious tests, seeking validation through how others treated me and what they offered. I expected them to intuitively understand my needs and desires, a flawed belief that led me through turbulent relationships and a few that were merely satisfactory.

My perspective shifted when I began focusing not on what I could receive from others, but on what I could contribute. This change was pivotal and transformed all my relationships. Today, I am preparing to marry my best friend, a uniquely wonderful man who values love and honesty as much as I do. Our shared commitment to generosity in love has enriched both our lives profoundly.

Nowhere is this lesson more poignant than in motherhood. My children, strong-willed and independent, have been my greatest teachers. While I wish I had always embraced this philosophy, parenting has been a journey of continual learning for me. Embracing the principle of allowing my loved ones to authentically be themselves has fostered open communication and nurtured the freedom for each of us to grow and evolve.

This process of self-discovery is dynamic, allowing us to uncover new facets of ourselves each day. Even on days when we falter and slip into old patterns of seeking validation from others, tomorrow offers the opportunity to rediscover and reaffirm who we truly are.

Choosing self-love and focusing on personal fulfillment are not selfish acts; they are the foundation of genuine, reciprocal love from others. Through my coaching experiences, I've come to understand and impart a crucial truth: every individual possesses the inherent wisdom and capacity to become more fully themselves. Each of us is already magnificent and capable of radiating our unique beauty into the world.

VIKKI ROOD

About Vikki Rood: Vikki Rood is a passionate advocate for joyful living, a seasoned empowerment coach, and a published author dedicated to helping individuals uncover their authentic selves and live lives filled with purpose, empowerment, and boundless joy. Vikki invites you to join her on a journey of self-discovery, empowerment, and joy.

Through coaching, workshops, and a thriving community, she'll help you uncover your authentic self, embrace your unique path, and find fulfillment in every facet of your life.

Author's Website: *www.VikkiRoodCoaching.com*

Book Series Website: *www.TheBookOfMentors.com*

WILLIAM BLAKE

MENTORSHIP BORN IN THE FIRE

"Don't wish it were easier; wish you were better."
~ Jim Rohn

Overcoming obstacles and building resilience are essential to becoming a phenomenal mentor. The toughest challenges we face often become our most valuable lessons, transforming our hardships into survival guides for others.

My journey with this lesson began in 2020, during the pandemic. My wife and I had just welcomed our first daughter and were enjoying every moment with her. Toward the end of that year, my wife, who has type 1 diabetes, started feeling constantly tired. Her endocrinologist noticed her thyroid was swollen and, after watching it for months, recommended lab tests. When they came back, we found she had thyroid cancer.

We caught it early enough to schedule surgery before it got worse. Initially, the plan was to remove only the left thyroid, but during the operation, the surgeon discovered the cancer had spread. They had to remove both sides of her thyroid. Thankfully, the cancer hadn't spread further, and my wife has been recovering well.

Looking back, I am in awe of how she continued to nurture our family despite her health challenges. She has battled type 1 diabetes since age two, had ankle surgery affecting her mobility, and was still healing from an emergency during our daughter's birth. Yet, every day, she shared a smile and cared for us.

My struggles during the pandemic seemed trivial in comparison. My wife's resilience profoundly inspired me. I am in awe of how she continues to face her challenges with grace and strength. To my wife, Makayla, your unwavering spirit and love are a constant source of inspiration to me.

Everyone faces challenges in life, but not everyone benefits from them. Some use their hardships as excuses, becoming victims. Others, like my wife, take their challenges in stride and emerge stronger and more inspiring.

There are three key differences between these two types of individuals. I want to share them with you, as they have transformed my own struggles into sources of strength. If you aspire to be a master mentor rather than just an average individual, let me share these three life-changing differences with you.

1. Mindset & Perspective

To transform your life, you must first transform your mindset. How we think shapes our reality, and getting this right is half the battle. Successful individuals view challenges as opportunities to learn and grow, while others see them as insurmountable barriers. In reality, the only thing truly stopping you is yourself.

When I launched my first business, I poured hours into minor tasks—spreadsheets, social media updates, and refining a program that no one had seen yet. I was enthusiastic about getting my first client, but it took me three months to get one. And it wasn't due to business scarcity; it was my dislike for sales.

I procrastinated, convinced that outside factors were to blame. It wasn't until I read Alex Hormozi's $100M Offers that I realized my inaction was the issue. Once I started reaching out, I landed my first client within three days. This experience taught me that challenges are opportunities in disguise and that action is key to overcoming obstacles. It all begins with the right mindset.

Similarly, my wife's battle with cancer and ongoing health issues embodies this principle. Despite her struggles, she maintained a positive outlook and continued to care for others. Her acceptance and resilience turned her challenges into sources of inspiration for many. To navigate life's hurdles, cultivate a mindset that embraces long-term growth. View challenges as chances to improve and you will discover the power to overcome even the toughest obstacles.

2. Resilience & Adaptability

Failure only occurs when you stop getting back up after falling. Many people view failure as a single moment when something goes wrong or when a mistake is made. I see it differently. To me, failure means one thing: you quit. That's it, plain and simple.

If you fall during a race but get back up, you're still in the race. If one business fails but you start another, you're still an entrepreneur. If you lose your temper as a parent but later apologize, you're still a good parent. The only true failure is giving up. As long as you keep getting up, striving to be better, and moving forward, you will achieve success. Success and failure are not opposites; success and learning are. Each time you rise after a fall, you learn and move forward.

Heroes, legends, and mentors master resilience and adaptability. They recover from setbacks, learn from their experiences, and persist. You can apply this mindset, too.

As long as you are better than you were yesterday, you are on the right path. Constant improvement, no matter how small, keeps you moving toward success. Remember David Bednar's words: "If I am better than I was yesterday, that is enough."

3. Support & Compassion

Support and compassion are vital for reclaiming your power and achieving your goals. While many may feel confident in their ability to offer support and compassion, there is always room for growth. To truly thrive and transform into a master mentor, you need a supportive community and a compassionate heart. Understanding and embracing these qualities will enable you to navigate life's challenges more effectively and inspire others to do the same.

Support is the village that nurtures and sustains you. The saying, "It takes a village to raise a child," holds true for anyone striving to be their best self. No Fortune 500 company reaches its heights with just one person; it takes a dedicated team. Similarly, we all need friends, family, and acquaintances to help us overcome obstacles and build resilience.

Compassion is just as important as support. In a world often viewed in black and white, reality is usually a shade of grey. Everyone faces challenges and could use a little more understanding. We all have stories, each in different chapters. As a mentor, it's crucial to approach others with compassion, recognizing that you are stepping into just one chapter of their lives. This perspective fosters a non-judgmental and supportive attitude, making you more effective in helping others.

Exceptional mentors understand the power of support and compassion. They use their experiences to empathize with and support others, creating a nurturing environment that promotes growth and resilience.

Rise Above the Fire & Lead

Now, it's up to you to decide: will you remain a mundane munchie or rise to be a master mentor? Witnessing my wife's incredible growth through her challenges has shown me that the difference between seeing yourself as a victim and using your challenges as opportunities lies in a simple choice. By adopting these three principles, you can improve yourself each day and live up to your fullest potential.

Through mindset and perspective, you learn to control your thoughts. Through resilience and adaptability, you harness that mental strength to guide your actions. And through support and compassion, you realize the world is bigger than just you, and we all need each other. These qualities forge heroes and legends in their own rights.

Choose to make a better life. Choose to be a better person. And always remember, as long as you are better than you were yesterday, that is enough. Embrace these principles and become the mentor you are meant to be. The world needs your unique strengths and experiences. Step up, make the choice, and lead others with wisdom, resilience, and compassion.

Take action today. Reflect on your mindset, build your resilience, and reach out to your support network. Your journey to becoming a master mentor starts now. The challenges you face are opportunities in disguise —embrace them and inspire others to do the same.

WILLIAM BLAKE

About William Blake: William is a speaker and motivator. He focuses on the skill sets of learning, listening, and observing to help people access new avenues of success and solutions. What might seem like regular everyday skills that most overlook, William teaches people how to find creative ways of accessing those skills.

William Blake is a stalwart professional in the world of organization, strategy, and methods. Being diagnosed with Dyslexia at a young age and struggling with reading and speaking, William is an example that through perseverance, any challenge can become a superpower.

William spearheads a dynamic coaching and speaking venture, empowering dyslexics to harness their unique strengths and embrace a world of boundless possibilities. He is also one of the chapter team leaders and corporate associates at Champion Circle Professional Association founded by Jon Kovach Jr.

From speaking to youth to being a camp counselor at Idaho Diabetes Youth Programs, William loves volunteering and helping children and teens believe in themselves and their unlimited potential. And of most importance to William is his love for his family. With his wife, he is dedicated to raising his daughters in a world of greatness, happiness, and unlimited belief.

Author's website: *www.WilliamBlakeLight.com*

Book Series Website: *www.TheBookOfMentors.com*

"LEARN TO BE THANKFUL FOR WHAT YOU ALREADY HAVE WHILE YOU PURSUE ALL THAT YOU WANT."

~ JIM ROHN

HABITUDE WARRIOR & INTEGRITY PUBLISHING EDITORIAL TEAM

Habitude Warrior International and Integrity Publishing take great pride in our editorial team who put their sweat, tears, and heart into each and every project and national bestseller! Thank you team!

JON KOVACH JR.
Team Manager

Jon Kovach Jr. strives to assist every author and every team member in the process of self-development for ultimate success.

PAT MINTON
VP of Operations

Pat Minton has been with the Habitude Warrior International team for over 20 years getting her start with Brian Tracy & Erik Swanson.

JILLIAN KOVACH
Editorial Manager

Jillian is a vital team member of Habitude Warrior & Integrity Publishing bringing her expertise managing our Editorial Department.

FATIMA HURD
Editorial Team & Photographer

Fatima is our Professional Photographer for Habitude Warrior as well as one of our members on the Proofing Department team.

LAUREN COBB
Editorial Team Member

Lauren Cobb is part of our Proofing Department for Habitude Warrior & Integrity Publishing as well as one of our authors.

To inquire about joining our team please send us an email to Team@HabitudeWarrior.com